Celebrity and the American Political Process

Integrated Marketing Communication

Series Editor: Jeanne M. Persuit,
University of North Carolina Wilmington

Integrated marketing communication (IMC) is a holistic approach to the areas of advertising, public relations, branding, promotions, event and experiential marketing, and related fields of strategic communication. This series seeks to ground IMC with communication ethics in order to take the theory and practice of IMC beyond a critical and deconstructive understanding and into new areas of productive inquiry. We seek to advance the scholarship of IMC in a manner that influences and informs future practice. Submissions may rely on varied methodologies and relate to the study and practice of communication and its theoretical diversity, including but not limited to the areas of rhetoric, visual communication, media ecology, philosophy of communication, mass communication, intercultural communication, and instructional communication. We welcome submissions addressing all facets of IMC and its relationship with communication ethics. While edited volumes will be considered, we encourage the submission of scholarly monographs that explore, in-depth, issues in IMC as related to communication ethics.

Titles in the series:
Celebrity and the American Political Process: Integrated Marketing Communication, by Jennifer Brubaker
Sport Teams, Fans, and Twitter: The Influence of Social Media on Relationships and Branding, by Brandi Watkins
Integrated Marketing Communication: Creating Spaces for Engagement, edited by Jeanne M. Persuit & Christina L. McDowell Marinchak

Celebrity and the American Political Process

Integrated Marketing Communication

Jennifer Brubaker

LEXINGTON BOOKS
Lanham • Boulder • New York • London

Published by Lexington Books
An imprint of The Rowman & Littlefield Publishing Group, Inc.
4501 Forbes Boulevard, Suite 200, Lanham, Maryland 20706
www.rowman.com

6 Tinworth Street, London SE11 5AL, United Kingdom

Copyright © 2021 The Rowman & Littlefield Publishing Group, Inc.

All rights reserved. No part of this book may be reproduced in any form or by any electronic or mechanical means, including information storage and retrieval systems, without written permission from the publisher, except by a reviewer who may quote passages in a review.

British Library Cataloguing in Publication Information Available

Library of Congress Cataloging-in-Publication Data

Names: Brubaker, Jennifer, 1976- author.
Title: Celebrity and the American political process : integrated marketing communication / Jennifer Brubaker.
Description: Lanham, Maryland : Lexington Books, 2020. | Series: Integrated marketing communication | Includes bibliographical references and index. | Summary: "This book uses an integrated marketing communication perspective to examine the brand of the celebrity as it is brought into the American political system, primarily in the form of celebrity endorsements"—Provided by publisher.
Identifiers: LCCN 2020030810 (print) | LCCN 2020030811 (ebook) | ISBN 9781498579728 (cloth) | ISBN 9781498579735 (epub)
Subjects: LCSH: Communication in politics—United States. | Advertising, Political—United States. | Endorsements in advertising—Political Aspects—United States. | Celebrities—Political activity—United States.
Classification: LCC JA85.2.U6 B78 2020 (print) | LCC JA85.2.U6 (ebook) | DDC 324.7/30973—dc23
LC record available at https://lccn.loc.gov/2020030810
LC ebook record available at https://lccn.loc.gov/2020030811

Contents

List of Figures — vii

Introduction — ix

PART I — 1

1 Integrated Marketing Communication — 3

2 Persuasion: Source Effects — 19

3 Persuasion: Receiver Effects — 33

PART II — 43

4 History of Celebrities and Politics — 45

5 Election 2016: The Celebrity Election — 63

6 Celebrities Post-2016: Everyone Is "Woke" — 79

Epilogue — 105

Appendix A: "It Doesn't Affect My Vote": A Study of Third-Person Effects of Celebrity Endorsements in the 2004, 2008, and 2012 Elections — 107

Index — 117

About the Author — 121

List of Figures

Figure 4.1	Charlie Chaplin, *The Great Dictator*, 1940	49
Figure 4.2	Ronald Reagan and General Electric Theater, 1954–62	52
Figure 4.3	Sammy Davis Jr. at Civil Rights March in Washington, 1963	53
Figure 4.4	Jane Fonda, 1975	54
Figure 4.5	"The Governator Ahh-nold"	57
Figure 4.6	2004 Vote for Change Concert in Washington DC, Featuring Dave Matthews, John Fogerty, Eddie Vedder, and Bruce Springsteen	59
Figure 5.1	Donald Trump, 2016, "Make America Great Again"	66
Figure 5.2	Jay Z and Friends Concert in Cleveland, 2016	72
Figure 6.1	San Francisco 49ers National Anthem Kneeling	91
Figure 6.2	President Donald Trump and Kanye West	99

Introduction

2004: the first post-9/11, post-hanging chad and dimpled ballots, post-weapons of mass destruction, post-Iraq War presidential election. As a country, we were in a different place than we had been four short years before. There was new sense of urgency. As ten Democrats sought the nomination to challenge President George W. Bush, the endorsements commenced. Beyond the typical newspaper and politician endorsements (e.g., former-VP Al Gore and Senator Ted Kennedy), celebrities began throwing their status behind the primary candidates. General Wesley Clark had the early support of the material girl herself, Madonna, documentarian Michael Moore and MASH's Alan Alda. Howard Dean had the support of TV's favorite sitting (in 2004) president, the West Wing's Jed Bartlett, also known as actor Martin Sheen, as well as Robin Williams and Susan Sarandon. But the strongest celebrity endorsements came in groups, as 2004 was a peak year for political activism movements, such as the established Rock the Vote campaign or the new Citizen Change organization. Both of these get-out-the-vote efforts used celebrities to target the eighteen- to twenty-nine-year-old voting demographic, using celebrity-filled PSAs and star-studded events to register voters, build enthusiasm, increase voter turnout, and, yes, often to endorse the celebrities' chosen candidates.

As a PhD student studying political communication, I was captivated by the campaign. As a twenty-something, I was right smack dab in the middle of Rock the Vote and Citizen Change's target demographic. And when Puff Daddy said "Vote of Die," he was talking to me. It was the political activism in these movements of celebrities like Dave Matthews, Bruce Springsteen, the Ruff Ryders, Lauryn Hill, Ashlee Simpson, and Natalie Portman that got me thinking and started this fifteen-year fascination that I've had with celebrities and politics. As that graduate student in 2004, I presented my first research on the role of celebrities in politics, "Great Expectations of Celebrities: Third-person Effects of Celebrity Endorsements." This book follows in the footsteps of that original study, as well as all of those that followed. Over the years, I have researched, presented, and published in numerous areas of political communication, with an emphasis on the interaction of media and politics, but the role of celebrity always manages to find a way in. As my interest in the celebrity-politics connection has grown, so has celebrity involvement in politics. What I first became interested in from a mere concert, PSA and/or the endorsement of a candidate here or there has grown beyond my wildest imagination to where we are in 2020, a time when celebrities are now criticized if they don't speak out on politics. They all have a political position, as well as the Instagram story to prove it. In 2020, celebrities are woke.

This book is the third in the Integrated Marketing Communication (IMC) series. It addresses the role of celebrity in American politics through an IMC perspective to examine the brand of celebrity and how this brand is brought into the American political system, primarily through celebrity endorsements and branding. The popularity and fame of celebrities are accompanied by the symbols and messages that they represent. Very similar to a product, this is their celebrity brand, and this brand, including their symbols and images, follows them in any medium in which they appear. Their brand becomes a heuristic cue for people, making assumptions when they see them.

People are increasingly taking their cues from celebrity activists. Celebrities sell—that's why they're celebrities. They have "it." Politics is a world of social networks, and celebrities can bring political causes and candidates their large networks, as well as the money and media attention that follows. A celebrity makes a particular candidate or cause stand out. In return, activism can bring a star both personal satisfaction and respectability.

The relationship between celebrities and political issues and social movements is evolving, and it is a significant time to look at this connection. In the past, it was a novelty to see the politically active celebrity, and the audience took notice. Today, it's becoming an expectation related to fame. It is more noticeable when a celebrity does not stand up for a cause, whether it's forcing athletes to take a stance (or a knee) during the national anthem or using celebrities' own stories of sexual harassment to encourage women to share their own sexual abuse or harassment on social media, it is now more than a norm—it's becoming a civic obligation associated with fame.

Despite this prominent and growing relationship, celebrities and American politics, especially as related to the celebrity brand, is an untapped area of research and discussion. Throughout part I of this book, we'll look at political celebrity branding, through the lens of both persuasion and IMC. In chapter 1, we discuss the evolving demands of society and the marketplace, as well as the resulting strategies for reaching publics and key stakeholders. Specifically, this book uses IMC to address the marketing and branding of politics, using celebrities as a strategy to reach voters.

IMC is a holistic approach to creating, distributing, and evaluating a common message to an organization's publics throughout all of its communicative efforts and platforms. The focus of IMC is to communicate one consistent strategic message to an audience. To accomplish this, IMC integrates an organization's advertising, public relations, and marketing techniques and strategies. Integrating these various functions into one holistic approach doesn't diminish the importance of any of them; rather, it emphasizes the strength and power they have when they are incorporated. IMC moved from marketing's business-oriented four Ps to focus on consumer-oriented four Cs. Unlike the traditional model where the primary focus is on the product and products are developed and pushed on the consumer, IMC's primary focus is on the consumer.

A key element in IMC is an organization's brand. A brand describes who you are and what you do through a combination of visual, verbal, tonal, and behavioral factors. Branding is the process of creating, maintaining, building, or changing a brand, and IMC maintains brand consistency by communicating a single clear, concise, and consistent brand through all messages and channels. Although more intangible than product brands, political leaders, organizations, parties, and movements also have brands. Political branding is how the public perceives that political leader or organization. When campaigning or once in office, political leaders are not only selling themselves, but they are selling their program ideas or policies. Establishing candidates' brand identity is a critical factor in determining whether they win or lose an election, and candidates with a strong brand will be much more effective. Similarly, movements and parties that successfully create and convey their brands to voters will more efficiently reach their target audiences. One strategy that is often used to reach audiences is celebrity branding or endorsements. While both celebrities and political leaders have brands, typically, the glitz and glamour of celebrity is more attention grabbing and holding than that of a political leader. For decades, voters have positively responded to celebrity endorsements of products. As with many commercial techniques, the effectiveness of celebrity endorsements was brought into the political realm. Commercially, celebrity endorsements are paid statements endorsing a product and are very effective. If endorsements are effective when the audience knows the celebrity is being paid, they become even more effective when, as with political endorsements, it appears that the celebrity is doing so without any personal gain. In politics, celebrity endorsements typically refer to a celebrity showing his or her endorsement of a candidate. Relatedly, celebrity branding uses the star's position of prominence, their brand due to fame and status, to draw attention to or start a conversation about a political issue. Both endorsements and branding use the celebrity's brand as a heuristic cue to raise the salience of a candidate or issue in the audience's mind. A celebrity acts as the brand's spokesperson and certifies the brand's claims and value by extending his or her fame, personality, popularity, or expertise to it. This IMC tactic uses the celebrity to transmit the political message, and give credence to it, to their adoring publics.

During an election season, voters face a multitude of political ads, speeches, news stories, and endorsements—both interpersonal and mediated—each day and are tasked with making a voting decision based on the information available and compiled from these sources. In chapter 2, we look at source effects—what is it about the source of persuasive messages that impacts its effectiveness, including how factors of the source fit into our processing of, elaboration on, and decisions about the persuasive messages we face each day? Celebrity brands impact these political messages when the celebrity becomes the source and their brand becomes a heuristic cue for receivers.

Two dual-process-based models of persuasion direct much of the research on the processing of political messages. The Elaboration Likelihood Model (ELM) and the Heuristic-Systematic Model (HSM) both assert that there are two different routes that individuals use to process persuasive communication messages, and that, from this, consumers formulate the attitudes that guide their behavior. The ELM expresses when individuals are more or less likely to think, or elaborate, on the arguments of a persuasive message. Based on the ELM, persuasive arguments will be processed through one of two routes, the central or the peripheral route, depending on mitigating factors. The key factors that determine processing route are motivation and ability. Persuasion research addresses when, or under what conditions, individuals are more likely to use one route over the other and what the persuasive effects are.

For individuals under high elaboration conditions, the success of persuasive messages will largely depend on the outcome, positive or negative, of their thoughtful consideration of the message content. However, for individuals under low levels of elaboration, who will not be carefully and thoughtfully considering the content of persuasive messages, the success of persuasive messages will often depend on other factors, primarily credibility, liking, and consensus. Credibility is partially based on dynamism, extroversion, and an overall charisma. Liking is partially based on physical attractiveness, and a facet of consensus is demonstrated through endorsement by others. Celebrities fit all of these. When a political figure or cause can gain celebrity endorsements, it demonstrates that others, namely attractive people who we like and deem credible, support them or their cause, merging credibility, liking and consensus, making celebrity itself a heuristic cue for low involvement individuals.

In chapter 3, we look at the receiver side of persuasive effects, addressing the way that the receiver perceives the message because of the source, by focusing on two persuasion concepts critical to understanding why celebrities can exert a persuasive influence, parasocial interaction, and third-person effects.

Parasocial interaction is a one-sided relationship or intimate friendship between a media consumer and a celebrity. These pseudo-relationships develop over time and include elements of involvement, intimacy, and even friendship. We consume the celebrities' tangible products (e.g., watching their movies, their TV shows, or their games; and listening to their music), we read about them in magazines and online, we see them in news stories and on entertainment news shows, and we follow them on social media. We see them in so many different ways that we feel like we know them. We are mentally participating in their lives, and we think and speak as if we are actually friends. Celebrities sell based off of this, so they often craft their brands in a way that we can imagine being friends with them. If our friends can be persuasive, convincing us to buy a product, support a cause or vote for a candidate, then so can our pseudo friends.

However, even though, like friends, they may be persuasive to us, we don't necessarily believe that we are so easily persuaded that we would make a purchase or cast a vote simply because a celebrity tells us to. Yet, while we don't believe that we'll be persuaded, we do still find them persuasive to others. The third-person effect predicts that people will overestimate the persuasive power of mass media messages on the attitudes and behaviors of others; whereas persuasive communication will not affect "you" or "me," it will affect "them," the third person. Social distance is a key variable, in that the greater the social distance between a person and a group, the greater the gap in the perceived impact of a persuasive message. Although we begin to look at third-person effects here, a deeper case study is presented in appendix A.

Throughout part II of this book, we move from the theory behind IMC and persuasion to focusing on the Hollywood-politics connection, historically through modern time. Chapter 4 looks at the history of celebrities and politics. Many of our earliest leaders, such as George Washington, used their celebrity, which came from military fame, to win office. Similarly, our earliest celebrities were these political leaders, as they were the only people who were famous. As technology progressed with the creation of photographs and the printing press, written and visual media, and the propensity for the audience to be drawn to it as entertainment, political leaders were the first to recognize and utilize its power and influence, depicting the early origins of celebrity or pop culture.

The Hollywood-Washington connection as we know it today is nothing new. Celebrities initially became attached to the Democratic Party and its causes in the 1930s. While we often associate celebrities with the left, the link between Hollywood and the conservative right was strong throughout the second half of the twentieth century. Whichever way they lean, Hollywood's biggest celebrities have become some of the most influential political activists. If a celebrity supports a cause or politician, then the public, the media, and policy-makers will take notice. Celebrities sell themselves, their music, and their movies. Celebrities sell the myriad of products that they endorse. In our celebrified culture, if they can sell all of that, they can sell a political candidate or cause. However, it must be considered that a shift to celebrity-driven activism depicts a fundamental shift of power in the United States, and potentially a simulated system of government.

The 2016 election of Donald Trump, a celebrity candidate with no prior political experience, demonstrated this shift driven by a celebrified culture. In chapter 5, we look at political marketing in the 2016 presidential election. As a former reality show host and paparazzi darling, Trump served as more of a celebrity than a politician during the campaign. If he wasn't enough celebrity, the 2016 election was flooded with celebrity endorsements—most on the Clinton side, as Clinton's celebrity endorsements topped Trump's in both numbers and star power. Clinton embraced these endorsements, whereas Trump eschewed them, despite his prior celebrity relationships during his pre-political years. Celebrities helped to fill the enthusiasm gap between Trump and Clinton, which was in favor of Trump throughout the entire campaign. If celebrities could inspire this group to get out and vote—and especially, to get out and vote for Clinton—it could have been a strategic advantage for her campaign.

But if celebrity endorsements work, as we discuss in the first four chapters, and Clinton had them in 2016, then why Trump? Celebrity endorsements were only ineffective on the Clinton side. Trump himself was the celebrity in his campaign. He used his celebrity as a means to reach and excite voters. Rather than traditional political marketing strategy, the market-driven politics of this campaign is highly representative of IMC. Trump changed political marketing. He took advantage of the shifting party-voter relationship, and managed to defy traditional calls for personal legitimacy and political credibility. The Trump campaign recognized the value of connective emotional themes, which appealed to a particular group of voters, providing him a path to victory. Trump categorically demonstrated the strength of a targeted consumer-based strategy, while Clinton took a more traditional candidate-driven campaigning approach.

Donald Trump, Hillary Clinton, and Bernie Sanders all have very distinct individual brands, as do the Democratic and Republican Parties. As part of his brand, Trump created a narrative that he was outside of the system, a wealthy businessman who couldn't be bought by special interests. Simultaneously, he crafted a narrative for the Clinton brand that she herself was the system. This tactic instilled loyalty and enthusiasm among these supporters and crafted a brand that Clinton couldn't escape. Perpetuating this narrative, Trump's brand took on a life of its own. He generated enthusiasm among supporters through a barrage of staged events, unprecedented usage of social media, and a reliance on earned and nontraditional media, won the election and successfully rebranded the Republican Party.

The Republican Party was in need of a rebrand, and Trump provided it. His candidacy brought with it a revolution. While Clinton's brand started and stopped at her, Trump (and Bernie Sanders) recognized that today's voters want more than a candidate. They want a movement. For Trump, his personality—his celebrity and his charisma—was his biggest attribute in inspiring a movement. In chapter 6, we look beyond 2016 to what has come after. In 2019, celebrities, with all of their personality and charisma, are both choosing to, and expected to, use their fame for political activism—much of which includes movements against Trump and his policies. And the closer we get to the 2020 election, we can already see celebrity involvement as a civic obligation. Activism has become a requirement of fame.

Celebrities have a large amount of resources, both money and attention, which, if applied correctly to a political movement, can generate a lot of attention and progress. But are these celebrities politically active or just politically vocal? Is it activism or opportunism? Mainstream culture has a way of commercializing a concept or trend, and then discarding it. And for celebrities, who have both the privilege and freedom to choose silence, when they choose to speak up, it is both morally satisfying and, often, professionally advantageous. Some celebrities are using their resources to launch movements and make significant change, such as Time's Up, #MeToo, and #BlackLivesMatter, and some are using their social media to show their followers just how #woke they are. For some, activism falls well within their celebrity brand, and therefore is a logical fit. But for others, it doesn't, so should it be a universal requirement for celebrities? Often, celebrity activists are a voice for positive change, but just as easily, a misstep can be magnified, hurting a cause. Celebrities have the ability to bring an issue to the top of the public consciousness, but how long will it stay there? Post-2016, we've seen socially conscious celebrities involve in the women's and Black Lives Matter movements, speak out pro-Trump and anti-Trump, lead boycotts, tackle bipartisanship, run for office, and even lend their brands to the growing legal marijuana industry. In each area, it's the celebrity's fame, followers, and media coverage of them that is so vast that whether or not they themselves have the ability to make any change or get any one person to vote a particular way or take action, they have influence. They draw attention and can help craft the media agenda, focusing on the issues that they deem important, which makes those issues the most salient in the minds of society.

In the epilogue, we'll discuss the first half of the 2020 presidential election, where celebrities are showing their support with their wallets, but withholding their candidate endorsements as the wide field flushes itself out. We finish with appendix A, an opportunity to return to the place this book began for me: 2004 and my first graduate school celebrity endorsement study, which I later expanded to include the elections of 2008 and 2012, as well. A few key findings emerged from this research, but the most important implication of this study was that, in an election filled with political polarization, when people are very strong in their political convictions and often unwavering in support of their presidential candidate and overall, political parties hold their bases, a celebrity endorsement supporting a candidate will not have any room to influence voters' decisions because they are already in favor of the endorsed candidate. However, including the concept of social distance, the in-group does have the potential to be persuaded by the opposing candidate's endorsements. As the 2020 race is sure to be one filled with both political polarization and celebrity endorsements, it is important to look at the patterns that have emerged in these recent elections to best assess the impact on current and future ones.

Part I

Chapter 1

Integrated Marketing Communication

As the demands of society and the marketplace change, so must strategies for reaching publics and key stakeholders. Whether it's an athletic brand, a travel destination, a retailer, or a political candidate or issue, creating a brand and promoting that brand to its various publics is critical to success. In the past, organizations employed a variety of functions to do this. In 1980, through the work of Schultz, Tannenbaum, and Lauterborn, integrated marketing communication (IMC) emerged as a field, combining both the business and communication aspects of these functions into one streamlined integrated and strategic method of communication (Du Plessis, van Heerden & Gordon, 2010; Persuit, 2014). Specifically, IMC is grounded in communication theory and connects marketing, public relations, and advertising (Bell McManus, Rouse & Verni, 2016). IMC is a holistic approach to creating, distributing, and evaluating a common message to an organization's publics throughout all of its communicative efforts and platforms.

> IMC is a strategic business process used to plan, develop, execute, and evaluate coordinated, measurable, persuasive brand communication programs over time with consumers, customers, prospects, and other targeted, relevant external and internal audiences. Although coming from a variety of vantage points, one message is consistently heard. (Persuit, 2014, p. 31; Schultz & Kitchen, 2000, pp. 20–21)

IMC recognizes the ongoing message exchange between the organization and the audience, grounding it in the communication discipline (McDowell Marinchak & Burk, 2016). From this communication perspective, the message itself is what is important. IMC places the communicative content of an organization into one strategic message, with the focus being placed on communicating that message with the audience (Persuit, 2014). The process of communicating this message includes multiple parts, all relevant and connected (Schultz & Kitchen, 1993). "IMC is the whole, and communication is the glue that holds all the parts together" (Bell McManus et al., 2016, p. 246). Through planning, one consistent and strategic message is delivered through multiple channels to establish long-term relationships and optimize specific communication objectives to lead to a desired behavior from the target audience (Bell McManus & Rouse, 2016). However, before moving on to how the fields are integrated, it is important to understand each field independently, with advertising and public relations coming from the communication side, and marketing stemming from business.

ADVERTISING AND PUBLIC RELATIONS

Advertising is a very controlled persuasive message, primarily distributed to the public through print, broadcast, or internet. The organization has complete control of its advertising because they pay for its distribution. Control is a strong benefit to the advertising function; however, audiences can be skeptical of ads because they know it is a persuasive message specifically designed to elicit a desired response from a targeted audience. When a consumer sees an advertisement for Coca Cola, Disney, Lincoln, or Hillary Clinton, they are receiving a controlled communication designed to convey a particular message and placed to most effectively reach a targeted audience. The message reaches the consumer exactly as intended by the organization because they have paid for it to do so. Advertising is a technical function that encourages potential consumers to choose a brand, product, service, movie, store, restaurant, or candidate over the other available options. Get your coffee at Starbucks rather than Dunkin'. Shop at Target instead of Walmart. Buy a Chevrolet, not a Ford or a Lincoln. Drink Fiji water, not Deer Park or Smart Water or Aquafina. Vote for Hillary Clinton, not Donald Trump. The primary goals of advertising are to reach consumers through the media, to expose them to a message, and to influence their attitudes, beliefs, and behaviors.

Sharing similar goals to advertising, public relations is more of a management function. It is a process of strategic communication intended to build a mutually beneficial relationship between an organization and its publics (Public Relations Society of America, 2019). From a public relations perspective, the message isn't controlled as with advertising, rather it is managed through research, actions, communication with the publics and evaluation (Marston, 2012). Like advertising, public relations also seeks to influence audiences, often through media, but it expands beyond a tangible purchase or vote type behavior to include engaging and building relationships with its key stakeholders, consumers, or publics. Through effective public relations, organizations are conscious of monitoring public opinion and policy and directing their decisions in ways to positively impact the future and their image.

Public relations seeks to promote the organization's social and citizenship responsibilities and protect its reputation. Facing a nationwide opioid epidemic, Blue Cross Blue Shield's "Painkillers Kill" awareness campaign showed the insurance company's social responsibility by raising awareness of the dangers of prescription medication. Oftentimes, it is through monitoring public opinion and policy that organizations make decisions on how to direct their public relations campaigns. Starbucks' announcement that they would eliminate single-use plastic straws by 2020 was in response to waste reduction initiatives. On their website, highlighting their social responsibility and strengthening their relationship with key stakeholders, Starbucks posted in their announcement:

> Starbucks decision to phase out single-use plastic straws is a shining example of the important role that companies can play in stemming the tide of ocean plastic. . . . We are grateful for Starbucks leadership in this space. . . . Starbucks has a 30-year track record of focusing on sustainability across all aspects of its business. (Starbucks, 2019)

Similarly, promoting awareness of gender issues, Burger King's "Proud Whopper" campaign included wrapping its Whoppers in a rainbow, in support of the Lesbian, Gay, Bisexual, Transgender, and Questioning/Queer (LGBTQ) community. In addition, Burger King heavily used social media to reach key stakeholders to gain attention and support for the issue and their campaign for social responsibility.

We'd be remiss to assume that public relations campaigns only aim to highlight an organization's social responsibility or protect its reputation. Public relations campaigns are often the precipice for raising awareness simply about the organization itself . . . or person himself, as was the case with Barack Obama's quick rise from relative obscurity in 2004 to the White House in 2008, which can be attributed to a successful public relations campaign. It was through a well-orchestrated public relations campaign, launched through extensive media efforts, from television appearances to magazine covers to news stories, and so on that the public even became aware of Barack Obama. Beginning with the strategic placement of him as the keynote speaker during the 2004 Democratic National Convention, the public's awareness was piqued. Afterward, he was highlighted on every type of media possible, moving him from virtual anonymity to the forefront. But it wasn't just his presence, or consumers' awareness of that presence, alone that made his campaign so successful. Key stakeholders still needed to be educated and persuaded, which were also key factors in Obama's public relations success. Similar to the response to public opinion by Starbucks and Burger King, Obama's public relations team was responsive to the public's needs and wants. Voters were responsive to his persuasive advertisements and messages, but in actuality, the successful public relations component was that voters' calls for "hope" and "change" were directly reflected in his persuasive messages, advertising, and rhetoric. Effective public relations campaigns like these monitor where key stakeholders stand and show how the individual or organization falls in relation.

MARKETING: FROM THE FOUR PS TO THE FOUR CS

If advertising and public relations are more the art side of IMC, marketing, from business, is the science component. Combining human psychology with scientific analysis (McManus, Rouse & Verni, 2016), marketing is a process that moves a product from concept to consumer. The primary goal of marketing is to develop a demand for a product in the eyes of potential consumers. This is accomplished by assessing the market needs and determining how best to satisfy the needs. An organization's marketing mix includes the management of four elements—or the four Ps of marketing—product, price, place, and promotion. As an organization follows its marketing plan from concept to consumer, it first identifies, selects, or develops the type of product—good or service—for which it believes there exists a consumer need or demand. Then, based on real and perceived value, supply and manufacturing costs, and competitors' pricing, the organization must determine the price that they determine consumers will pay. Awareness comes in again here with place because consumers need to be aware of the product; consumers can't or won't buy products that they don't know exist, so organizations must determine where best to place its product, where to sell it and/or how to deliver the product to the marketplace by selecting an appropriate distribution channel. Last, promotion brings in the advertising and public relation elements as the organization develops and implements a promotional strategy to show consumers why they need this product and what they should pay for it.

Integrating the various functions (advertising, public relations, and marketing) into one holistic approach doesn't diminish the importance of any of them; rather, it emphasizes the strength and power they have when they are incorporated. Similar to Gestalt theory, IMC follows the adage "the whole is greater than the sum of its parts." While the fields of marketing, public relations, and advertising can successfully stand alone, when integrated, they create a stronger and more distinctive message (Bell McManus & Rouse,

2016), and it is communication that binds these independent fields together into IMC.

If marketing also brings in the advertising and public relations elements to some degree already, one might question how traditional marketing differs from IMC. Whereas traditionally, marketing focuses on attitudes, IMC focuses on consumer behavior, believing that behavior is a more reliable and measurable metric, and that past behavior is more indicative of future behavior than simply looking at consumer attitudes (Persuit, 2014). IMC moved from marketing's business-oriented four Ps to focus on consumer-oriented four Cs—consumer, cost, convenience, and communication. Unlike the traditional model where the primary focus is on the product and products are developed and pushed on the consumer, IMC's primary focus is on the consumer. Consumer behavior is studied and market research is applied, and products are developed based on the consumer's demand. While cost is comparable to price in the traditional model, it differs in that IMC again looks at the consumer rather than the product. What value does the consumer place on the product? What cost is the consumer willing to pay, as opposed to what does it cost to produce the product? To successfully market to consumers, the product must be conveniently placed. Similar to placement, all aspects from purchase to delivery to installation must be convenient for the consumer. As opposed to the traditional marketing focus of promotion, IMC places high value on the brand, specifically, communication of the brand to create a brand awareness and brand recognition. Knowing the most effective communication strategies and methods for segmenting, targeting, and positioning your product based on the brand and your target audience for that brand is crucial to success.

BRAND AND BRANDING AS PART OF IMC

Every business, organization, and person has a brand. You have a brand. Starbucks and Target have brands. Your favorite celebrity has a brand. Your city has a brand. Our president has a brand. A brand is the overall impression presented outward, and everyone wants their brand to be valued by others. It's the perception of your company, products, and services in people's minds. A brand is how consumers think and feel about who you are as an organization and what you do. A brand describes who you are and what you do through a combination of visual, verbal, tonal, and behavioral factors, including your name, what you do, sell, or provide, how you convey yourself through your written and oral communication, your social media presence, your logo, your colors, your packaging or physical appearance, your location, your advertising, your sound, your voice. It is how people identify, know, and remember you and distinguish you from others, including from competitors or rivals. Brands are overall narratives, including logo, consistent visual images and a few specific selling points about the product (Cosgrove, 2009). Brand communication is how that brand is communicated to the public, and IMC ensures that a single clear, concise, and consistent brand is presented through all messages and channels.

As a marketing strategy, *branding, or brand development, is the process of creating, maintaining, building, or changing a brand, and IMC maintains brand consistency throughout all media and communication functions. An overall goal of branding in IMC is to* acquire loyal customers who are happy with the quality and benefits of the brand and are therefore willing to support the organization, whether it is through use, purchase, patronage, or vote. The brand development process involves positioning your organization in the market, developing a brand strategy to grow and reach your goals, creating your verbal and visual identities, writing verbal messages, and creating and maintaining an IMC plan for keeping your brand consistent.

POLITICAL MARKETING

Often, when we talk about marketing techniques and politics, we hear criticisms such as, "are we marketing our president like we do a brand of toothpaste?" While we'd probably prefer to think we're not, political marketers use many of the same strategies and techniques when marketing political candidates and causes as they do commercial products. All persuasion efforts have the same goal: to successfully influence a target audience's behavior to a recommended course of action. That recommended course of action may be to purchase a brand of toothpaste, or to shop at a store, or to go see a movie, or to vote for a candidate. Many tools, techniques, and concepts cross over from commercial marketing to political marketing. The primary difference is that rather than goods and services, political marketing promotes critical issues and leadership choices within the country, state, and local community.

While the candidates we vote for and the causes we support may be based on how well the platforms of each of the candidates align with our own beliefs and values, it is more likely that our votes and support are also based on the outcomes of carefully targeted political marketing campaigns. Political marketing involves the ways that "political elites use marketing tools and concepts to understand, respond to, involve and communicate with their political market in order to achieve their goals" (Lees-Marshment, 2014, p. 2). The most obvious political goal, of course, is to win or to get votes, but sometimes a political goal might be more intangible, long term, or values based. Political marketing may work to attain goals that involve political causes or issues rather than individuals, such as getting an item on the political agenda, gaining support for an issue, bringing awareness to a cause, passing legislation, or stimulating action. Political marketing may have more societal goals, such as increasing political participation, voter turnout, and political knowledge or making the world a better place. Regardless of the political goal, its tangibility or loftiness, the only way to hope to achieve these goals is through reaching stakeholders and influencing their beliefs, attitudes, and behaviors to align with the intent of the marketer.

Political action depends on a variety of key stakeholders, including all of those invested in, interested in, or impacted by the party, candidate, or issue. This market is wide reaching, as it is comprised of citizens, voters, party members, donors and potential donors, staff, candidates, politicians, lobbyists, regulatory bodies, and the media (Lees-Marshment, 2014). When marketing, politicians must identify, target, and take care of these stakeholders for political success. The modern political marketing landscape provides innumerable opportunities and tools to connect with key stakeholders, shape public opinion, and influence behavior. In recent decades, traditional methods of outreach, such as direct mail, cold calls, face-to-face interaction, television, radio, and print, have been expanded to include email, texting, talk show/entertainment appearances, and social media outreach. With all of these channels available, political marketing campaign messages are quickly and easily consumed by and diffused among stakeholders, creating an organic environment for raising awareness, educating, and influencing behavior.

To create and diffuse campaign messages and ultimately influence behavior, political elites are increasingly using techniques pervasive in commercial marketing. Political marketing provides a variety of functional implements to reach stakeholder audiences and achieve political goals, including research, strategic, organizational, and communication tools (Lees-Marshment, 2014). Political marketers need to do thorough research on their audience and opposition and can employ the use of various marketing tools and methods, qualitative and quantitative, formal and informal, for candidates, parties, organizations, and governments to understand the political marketplace. To gather information about the attitudes, beliefs, behaviors, needs, and wants of the public and key stakeholders, political market research includes a combination of quantitative tools, such as polls, surveys, voter profiling, segmentation, big data and analytics, qualitative tools, such as focus groups, interviews, opposition, and policy research, and other information, such as public records data. Based off of this research, the campaign can make decisions about strategy, brand, policies, and communication with their publics to inform, educate, persuade, and influence attitudes and behaviors.

POLITICAL BRANDING

Just as every product has a brand, political leaders and organizations also have brands, and they must be aware of their strengths and weaknesses, working to promote themselves with their strengths and diminish or improve on their weaknesses (Lees-Marshment, 2014). Political branding is how the public perceives that political leader or organization. Political brands are more intangible than product brands; they are more feelings about, impressions of, or associations with that leader or organization that distinguish them from others in the eyes of voters or the public. Political branding allows the political entity to "change or maintain reputation and support, create a feeling of identity with the party or its candidates to create a trusting relationship between political elites and consumers" (Lees-Marshment, 2014, p. 104). It's a quick way for audiences to understand and process an overall perception of the political image of a political candidate, campaign, party, policy, organization.

Unlike commercial branding, political branding involves the commodification of people and ideas, not simply products and services. Political branding goes beyond the superficial and also informs how policies are sold to the public, how the United States engages in diplomacy around the world, and how people identify with political parties. While the political brands may be intangible, they are just as valuable. During elections, the candidates are positioned as products themselves. Establishing candidates' brand identity is a critical factor in determining whether they win or lose an election, and candidates with a strong brand will be much more successful. The branding of a political leader includes providing stakeholders with a simple yet distinctive vision, depicting their values and positions to gain a strong awareness among voters to stimulate positive associations (Lees-Marshment, 2014).

Political leaders need to develop a positive brand personality and convey that brand personality to their various publics. That brand develops from a combination of observed behaviors and inferences made based on actions or statements of intended actions (Lee-Marshment, 2014). Smith (2009) suggested six important components of a political brand personality: honesty, spirit, image, leadership, toughness, and uniqueness. Similarly, Guzman and Vicenta (2009) proposed three principles of effective brand personality: capability, openness, and empathy. This suggests that political leaders must create and perpetuate a brand that displays a combination of credibility characteristics (i.e., image and openness), values characteristics (i.e., honesty and empathy), and leadership characteristics (i.e., toughness and capability).

When campaigning or once in office, political leaders are not only selling themselves, but they are selling their program ideas or policies. To help gain support from Congress, lobbyists, voters, and the media, political branding can help political leaders gain needed support to get legislation passed to follow through on campaign promises (Lees-Marshment, 2014). Barberio (2006) outlined three principles of successful policy branding. First, the policy should be branded to appeal to universally desired values, such as strength, reliability, and fairness. Second, branding should make claims about the policy that offer a comparison between it and the competing policy, showing its superiority in satisfying those desired values. Last, branding of policy should encourage the stakeholders to see benefits beyond those immediately evident in the policy. Successful examples of presidential policy brands include "The New Deal," "No Child Left Behind," and "The Affordable Care Act."

Political movements also benefit from strong political branding efforts. The women's movement, the civil rights movement, the AIDS Rebellion, the Tea Party Movement, the Occupy Wall Street Movement, and Black Lives Matter are just a few examples of branded political movements. The success of a political movement is partly due to how they use branding to help citizens understand their goals and functions, using memorable tactics that play on related beliefs of individuals (Lees-Marshment, 2014).

Similarly, political parties also need to have effective brands. Effective political party branding can have rippling impacts as it helps political leaders succeed in presidential, national, and statewide elections (Lees-Marshment, 2014). Branding allows political parties to present their ideas clearly and concisely to voters to efficiently hit their target audiences. Conley (2012) presented five principles of successful party branding, including conducting market research, designing brand concepts to create a brand based on market demand, implementing the party brand to coordinate the parties activities, communicating and managing the brand with its target audiences and delivering on the party's promises, ideals, and images in its governing to create brand loyalty. Cosgrove (2007) argued the success of Branded Conservatives with a branding of their movement and party helping them dominate in American politics from 1980 to 2008. Ronald Reagan was the face of the Conservative Brand, using his celebrity status and techniques to be the brand's biggest salesman (Cosgrove, 2007). The branding of Conservatism with Ronald Reagan at its forefront is one or the most historic, visible, and organic examples of the relationship between celebrity and political branding.

CELEBRITY BRANDING AND CELEBRITY ENDORSEMENTS

Celebrity branding and endorsements are separate yet entwined concepts that often overlap in both commercial and political marketing, as marketers recognize the impact celebrities can have on the sales or popularity of a product, a candidate or a cause. Celebrity branding uses the celebrity's position of prominence to start a conversation, whereas celebrity endorsements are the traditional (often paid) statement endorsing a product. In politics, celebrities use their brand to support their endorsements of a candidate or cause.

Celebrities are branded in a similar way to political candidates, with a value placed on their social lives, endorsements, and related products, such as movies or music. The celebrity brand is a shortcut, a heuristic cue, that allows the public to use their feelings about or impressions of the celebrity as a way to compare them to other celebrities in their minds. Political branding intersects with celebrity branding when a politician, policy, or movement links their brand to the celebrity's brand in an attempt to use the celebrity's status to promote itself or its cause.

Relatedly, celebrity endorsement attaches the fame of a celebrity to a product, or in the case of political marketing, a candidate, party, policy or movement. The popularity of the celebrity is used to an advantage. Audiences often consider celebrities to be role models of sorts, and they like to do things and buy products that celebrities do or use. Celebrity endorsements are an IMC tactic that capitalizes on this adoration. The celebrity acts as the brand's spokesperson and certifies the brand's claims and value by extending his or her fame, personality, popularity, or expertise to the brand. In a market where consumers are faced with a very high propagation of options, celebrity endorsement is a way to provide a distinct differentiation among them. In a celebrity endorsement, the celebrity becomes the face of the brand message. The brand has a message, and the celebrity helps convey that message to their publics. Consumers see the celebrity as a channel transmitting the message directly from the brand to them.

Political marketing takes this tactic and applies it to political candidates, policy, or movements. Again, the celebrity acts as a proxy for the candidate, using his or her own notoriety and position in the public consciousness as a way to validate the political claims being made, certifying their importance, relevance, and authenticity in the minds of the voters. Celebrities again serve as a channel, transmitting the political message, and giving credence to it, to their adoring publics. In a sea of politicians and political causes, the celebrity endorser draws attention to that one in particular, making it distinctive in the public eye. The celebrity lends his or her fame and credibility to the political candidate or cause, just as they would a pair of shoes, a car, a watch, or a bottle of shampoo. If markets will buy a pair of shoes because of LeBron James, a car because of Matthew McConaughey, a watch because of George Clooney, or a shampoo because of Jennifer Aniston, they'll also be attracted to a cause or support a political candidate because of their celebrity endorsement of it.

The success of a celebrity endorsement depends on a number of factors. First, the celebrity must be attractive to audiences. If audiences find the celebrity attractive, it will have a positive impact on the endorsed brand. Celebrities are typically attractive in their appearance, talents, intellect, athletic capabilities, and lifestyle. People like attractive people. When you like someone, you are more likely to follow their recommended course of action, which is why liking is a critical factor in persuasion. Second, the celebrity must have some degree of real or perceived credibility. Credibility can very simply be defined as the perceived believability of a source by the audience. It also refers to their charisma, a lay term to describe someone who possesses an indefinable charm or allure—something celebrities have in abundance, which is part of what makes them celebrities. More specifically, credibility includes expertise, trustworthiness, and goodwill. When audiences are faced with a proliferation of brands, attaching the credibility of a celebrity to one brand sets it apart and gives it an advantage over other brands. Similarly, when faced with multiple political candidates, that same celebrity attachment sets a candidate apart from the rest, giving him or her an advantage. Last, a celebrity endorsement is most successful when there is an organic compatibility between the celebrity and the brand. For example, LeBron James endorsing basketball shoes is a highly compatible match, but LeBron endorsing Intel doesn't have the same degree of authenticity. As a woman, Reese Witherspoon's work promoting feminism has a natural compatibility for advocacy, as does LeBron James', as an African American, activism for Black Lives Matter.

MEANING TRANSFER PERSPECTIVE AND HALO EFFECT

Audiences attribute the positive qualities or characteristics of celebrities to the products, political candidates, or causes they endorse. All of the good that audiences bestow on the celebrities, by proxy, transfers through the endorsement. Meaning Transfer Perspective describes the process of how celebrities acquire their brand and then transfer that brand to the products they endorse. An endorser's public persona is projected onto a product, and the product's image is then incorporated into the consumer's self-concept. The celebrity brand—ideally, celebrity credibility—is subconsciously transferred to the brand. Use of the right celebrity can accelerate brand-building more quickly than a marketing plan not using it, which is a marketing shortcut, as it increases consumer trust and awareness.

An extension of the halo effect, the goal is to take the celebrity charisma and have it transfer to the endorsed. The halo effect is a cognitive bias in our processing of information, in which one part makes the whole seem better. We take a mental shortcut and extrapolate that when one dimension of an individual is positive, others must be as well. If a person is well liked, he or she will be rated as being very high or positive on all other specific traits, even if they are unrelated (Krech, Crutchfield & Ballachey, 1962). In today's culture, celebrities are some of the most well-liked people out there, leading to many opportunities for a halo effect. She's a beautiful model, so I find the clothes she wears beautiful, and I will want to own them myself. He's a great basketball player, so his shoes must be great. I like his movies, so I will like his political picks. Her music speaks to me, so her politics do too. Rationally, we know that one factor doesn't lead to the other, but the shortcuts we take when processing all of the information we are constantly bombarded with leads us to fall for it.

CELEBRITY INFLUENCE MARKETING

Today's celebrities are also taking a more covert role in marketing with celebrity influence marketing. Related to celebrity branding and endorsements, influence marketing creates word-of-mouth advertising using people who are trusted in certain circles. Similar to endorsements, the sources are perceived to be credible, and they use that credibility to create a buzz among their followers. Some of these endorsers are celebrities in other areas as well as being looked at as influential, while others are only known for being influencers. The influencers can build up the brand of a product, politician, or cause to their followers. In a celebrity endorsement, communication is one way, using mediated channels, one to many. Celebrity endorsements are meant to be seen and heard, but not to be interacted with. In influence marketing, the whole goal is to interact. The endorsement is part of an ongoing dialog that the influencer has with his or her followers. The brand, product, politician, or cause is woven into the ongoing narrative that their followers are already invested in. As followers, we might see a celebrity promote her new movie, a magazine cover shoot, a supplement she uses (product endorsement), pictures of her children, her dinner, and her political activism—all as part of an ongoing story that, as followers, we are heavily connected to. When audiences see typical advertisements, it's assumed that it is created content made specifically with a persuasive intent. However, in influence marketing, audiences perceive that the influencer is actually the creator of the message, and that he or she is speaking to us. This perception of originality lends it more authenticity and credibility than more formal types of advertising, feeling more natural, organic, and direct than a more formal endorsement.

WHEN CELEBRITY BRANDING GOES WRONG

Sometimes, celebrity endorsements can turn bad. Tiger Woods. Paula Deen. Kate Moss. Michael Phelps. Mel Gibson. Kathy Griffin. All have, at one time or another, been both the poster child, and quickly turned black sheep, of a brand. Whether it's because of an unpopular political opinion or a celebrity gone bad, if a celebrity can transfer their good to a brand, their bad can transfer as well, and both corporations and candidates want to distance themselves from that negative attention as quickly as possible.

Drug use, publicly cheating on your spouse, a racist or homophobic rant, or an arrest, celebrities can fall on hard times after taking a big public relations hit. In an effort to mitigate the situation, associated brands need to ask, what's the collateral damage? For both products and political campaigns, unwanted baggage on their endorser can be a huge public relations and financial disaster as they need to manage the public backlash. The brand may choose to end the relationship with the celebrity to protect themselves. Brands need to determine the long-term relationship and implications and then decide how to proceed. While ending the relationship with the accused endorser may reduce immediate backlash on the brand, once the scandal blows over, brands may find it more beneficial, long term, to have stuck with the endorser. After Tiger Woods' infidelities became public, brands such as Gillette, General Motors, and Gatorade ended his endorsements to protect themselves, while Nike opted to ride out the scandal and keep him on, despite their dropping sales. Years later, Tiger is back on top, and he is still winning championships in his Nike gear.

A benefit of celebrity endorsers is that they have wide reach throughout the media and are often unscripted, which adds to the authenticity. What happens when they go off-script? Political campaigns especially want endorsers to stay on target with their message. During the 2016 election, Susan Sarandon made risky assertions and launched her own political attacks. Actor Tim Robbins tweeted out inaccurate exit poll information favoring Bernie Sanders in the primary; and Rosario Dawson, another Sanders' supporter, made mention of Monica Lewinsky in a reference to bullying and suggested the Clinton campaign was engaging in the same type of behavior. Bernie Sanders stated, "We have many, many surrogates who say many, many things. Many of these surrogates do not agree with everything I say. And I do not agree with every approach and everything that they say. And that's the simple reality."

REBRANDING

To remain successful, products, organizations, cities, political leaders, and political parties need to respond to the environment and change over time. Rebranding can involve a full rebrand, redefining the entire brand identity, or a partial rebrand, focusing on a refresh or update. Sometimes celebrities can help a product rebrand. In 2014, Lincoln was looking for a partial rebrand, primarily to place them in a different demographic as they promoted a new crossover vehicle, so they brought in Matthew McConaughey as a celebrity endorser. The outlandish commercials coupled with his distinct celebrity image spurred numerous parodies and a good deal of buzz, leading to a successful rebrand and a surge in sales. A total rebrand is needed when an organization undergoes a total change in identity. Rebranding in politics may be necessary when a brand has attracted negative attention or when a leader or party wants to head in a different direction (Lees-Marshment, 2014). While typically long-standing, political brands often need a partial rebrand; however, the attachment many feel with a political brand can make it highly difficult to change. In chapter 5, we'll look at how Trump rebranded the Republican Party in 2016.

BRANDS CAPITALIZING ON POLITICAL MOVEMENTS

Historically, companies have aimed to remain apolitical, fearful of taking a political stance and damaging their market share. However, since the 2016 election, brands have begun to intentionally link themselves to a social or political movement in an effort to express their values and societal commitments, as well as capitalize on related sales. According to Edelman's Earned Brand Study (2018), 57 percent of consumers will buy or boycott a brand because of its position on an issue, and 65 percent of consumers will not buy a brand when it chooses to stay silent on an issue they feel it has an obligation to address. Brands are noting that consumers are no longer only purchasing a product based on quality; they are belief-driven buyers who shop with a conscience. Similarly, voters have become belief driven, and in chapter 5, we'll discuss the role that played in the 2016 election.

REFERENCES

Barberio, R.P. (2006). "Branding: Presidential politics and crafter political communications." Paper presented at the *2006 Annual Meeting of the American Political Science Association*, Philadelphia, PA.

Bell McManus, L.M. & Rouse, C. (2016). "Integrated marketing communication and event planning: An academic conference in the Charm City." In Jeanne M. Persuit & Christina L. McDowell Marinchak (eds.), *Integrated Marketing Communication: Creating Spaces for Engagement*. Lanham, MD: Lexington, 37–52.

Bell McManus, L.M., Rouse, C. & Verni, S. (2016). *Event Planning: Communicating Theory and Practice*. Dubuque, IA: Kendall Hunt.

Clio Awards. (2019). *Burger King: Proud Whopper*. Retrieved April 22, 2019 from https://clios.com/awards/winner/public-relations/burger-king/proud-whopper-548.

CNN. (2019). *Starbucks Strawless Cup*. Retrieved April 22, 2019 from http://money.cnn.com.

Conley, B.M. (2012). "The politics of hope: The democratic party and the institutionalization of the Obama brand in the 2010 mid-term elections." In Jennifer Lees-Marshment (ed.), *Routledge Handbook of Political Marketing*. New York, NY: Routledge, 124–135.

Cosgrove, K.M. (2007). "Midterm marketing: An examination of marketing strategies in the 2006, 2002, 1998 and 1994 elections." Paper presented at the *Annual Meeting of the American Political Science Association*. Retrieved January 12, 2019 from http://www.allacademic.com/meta/p209749_index.html.

Cosgrove, K.M. (2009). "Case study 5.4: Branded American politics." In Jennifer Lees-Marshment (ed.), *Political Marketing: Principles and Applications*. London and New York, NY: Routledge, 107–123.

Du Plessis, F., van Heerden, N. & Gordon, C. (2010). *Integrated Marketing Communication* (3rd ed.). Pretoria: Van Schaik Publishers.

Edelman's Earned Brand Study. (2018). *Brands Take a Stand*. Retrieved January 25, 2019 from https://www.edelman.com/earned-brand.

Guzman, F. & Vicenta, S. (2009). "A political candidate's brand image scale: Are political candidates brands?" *Journal of Brand Management*, 17(3): 207–217.

Krech, D., Crutchfield, R.S. & Ballachey, E.L. (1962). *Individual in Society: A Textbook of Social Psychology*. New York, NY: Mcgraw Hill.

Lees-Marshment, J. (2014). *Political Marketing: Principles and Applications*. London and New York, NY: Routledge.

The Lincoln Motor Company. (2014). *Bull*. Retrieved April 26, 2019 from https://www.lincoln.com/luxury-crossovers/mkc/.

Marston, J. (2012). *The Nature of Public Relations*. Whitefish, MT: Literary Licensing.

McDowell Marinchak, C.L. & Burk, J.K. (2016). "Engaged communicative consumption: How IMC campaigns generate a space for civic conversation." In Jeanne M. Persuit & Christina L. McDowell Marinchak (eds.), *Integrated Marketing Communication: Creating Spaces for Engagement*. Lanham, MD: Lexington, 7–22.

Persuit, J.M. (2014). *Social Media and Integrated Marketing Communication: A Rhetorical Approach*. Lanham, MD: Lexington.

Public Relations Society of America. (2019). *What is Public Relations?* Retrieved January 18, 2019 from https://www.prsa.org/all-about-pr/.

Schultz, D.E. & Kitchen, P.J. (2000). *Communicating Globally: An Integrated Marketing Approach.* Chicago, IL: NTC/Contemporary Publishing Group.

Smith, G. (2009). "Conceptualizing and testing brand personality in British politics." *Journal of Political Marketing,* 8(3): 209–232.

Starbucks. (2019). *Starbucks to Eliminate Plastic Straws Globally by 2020.* Retrieved April 24, 2019 from https://stories.starbucks.com/press/2018/starbucks-to-eliminate-plastic-straws-globally-by-2020/.

Chapter 2

Persuasion

Source Effects

In today's political climate, we, as media consumers, are faced with a multitude of political messages. Just checking Facebook alone, we see countless posts from the political figures that we follow, news articles from a variety of media organizations, political commentary from both our "friends" and an assortment of celebrities, whether actors, musicians, or athletes. And that is on an average day, months out from a midterm election. Just look through your feed. Among the vacation photos and animal videos, you'll be amazed at how little does not have political undertones, if not blatant overtones.

During the 2016 election, $6.4 billion was spent on political ads by candidates, political parties, and interest groups (Open Secrets Center for Responsive Politics, 2017). In addition to the political ads, during a campaigning season, voters face a multitude of speeches, news stories, and endorsements—both interpersonal and mediated—each day and are tasked with making a voting decision based on the information available and compiled from these sources. And this all is within an already cluttered commercial media environment, in which consumers are exposed to over 10,000 persuasive brand messages each day, brand messages that force us to make decisions about every product we purchase, service we use, place we go, and opinion we hold. How do we process all of these messages? We process some messages with careful thought and others without any real deliberation. What factors impact which messages we process in which way?

Persuasion research addresses four types of effects that impact the persuasiveness of messages: source, receiver, channel, and message. The source, either direct or indirect, refers to the person or persons communicating the message, and source effects refer to what aspects of that source make a message more or less persuasive. The receiver refers to the person who is the recipient of the persuasive message, and receiver effects refer to what characteristics or factors impact how the receiver responds to the persuasive message. Channel refers to the various ways that persuasive messages are distributed (i.e., interpersonally—face to face, text, email, social media—or mediated—TV, print, radio, social media), and channel effects address what channels are most effective at transmitting which types of messages and why. Message effects refer to the message itself, including the content and structure that impact persuasiveness.

In its discussion about processing persuasive message, this chapter will touch on source effects—what is it about the source of persuasive messages that impacts its effectiveness? Specifically, what factors about the source fit into our processing of, elaboration on, and decisions about the persuasive messages we face each day? What impact do celebrities and their brand have on messages when they become the source and their brand becomes a heuristic cue for receivers who make assumptions based on that brand when they hear the message transmitted from them? And what about when these messages happen to be political?

DUAL-PROCESS MODELS AND PERSUASIVE MESSAGES: ELABORATION LIKELIHOOD MODEL

As with other types of persuasive messages, political messages are processed in different ways, depending on a number of factors. Two process-based models of persuasion direct much of the research in the field. The Elaboration Likelihood Model (ELM), formulated by Richard E. Petty and John C. Cacioppo, and the Heuristic-Systematic Model (HSM), conceived by Shelly Chaiken and Alice H. Eagly, are both dual-process models that assert that there are two different routes that individuals use to process persuasive communication messages. From this, consumers formulate the attitudes that guide their behavior.

The ELM is centered around the notion that individuals are in a variety of contexts and working under different conditions, so they will not all process information in the same way (Petty & Cacioppo, 1986). Elaboration refers to the issue-related thoughts about the arguments proposed in the persuasive message, and it is assumed to fall along a continuum, ranging from considerable attention to the central arguments of a message to relatively little thought processing about the message. The model conveys when individuals are more or less likely to think, or elaborate, on the arguments of a persuasive message. Persuasion can occur at any point along this elaboration continuum.

Based on the ELM, persuasive arguments will be processed through one of two routes, the central or the peripheral route, depending on mitigating factors. The central route involves an individual applying careful consideration as they evaluate the arguments proposed in the message. They compare these thoughts to their individual beliefs, as they evaluate their attitudes and make decisions regarding their behavior. The central route involves carefully thinking about and considering a message's arguments. Comparatively, the peripheral route involves much less deliberation. Instead of examining the arguments, individuals focus on quick and easy features or cues to aid in decision-making regarding whether to accept or reject the message. Peripheral cues provide something simple to focus on, rather than the complexities of the arguments. Peripheral cues might involve such things as the physical appearance of the speaker, the fun atmosphere created in the advertisement, or the familiarity of a candidate's name. When the central route is used, attitude change will be more enduring and more predictive of behavior, as individuals will have used more cognitive effort and become more involved in the arguments; however, when the peripheral route is used, attitude change will be both temporary and less predictive of behavior, as individuals will be less invested in the argument (Petty & Cacioppo, 1983).

Individuals are capable of being both central and peripheral processors. Persuasion research addresses when, or under what conditions, individuals are more likely to use one route over the other and what the persuasive effects are. The key factors that determine processing route are motivation and ability. In order to use the central processing route, an individual must possess both the motivation to thoughtfully attend to the arguments in the message and the ability to process them. If either of these factors is lacking, the individual will rely on peripheral cues to make a decision. High elaboration will occur, and issue-related arguments processed, when the consumer is both motivated and able. Consequently, the attitudes shaped under this high elaboration will be more predictive of behavioral intention and behavior and be more resistant to counter-persuasive argument (Petty, Cacioppo & Schumann, 1983; Verplanken, 1991). Persuaders can ascertain that their persuasive arguments processed via the central route (high elaboration) will be more persistent over time and more resistant to counterarguments than low elaboration (peripheral route) processing.

FACTORS INFLUENCING ELABORATION AND ROUTE: MOTIVATION

Two main factors determine the amount of elaboration an individual will apply to the processing of a persuasive argument, and, therefore, the route to persuasion that individual will take: motivation and ability. A receiver will only be capable of using the central route for processing a persuasive message if that individual is motivated to carefully attend to the arguments, as well as able to engage in thoughtful elaboration. Although a variety of factors have been researched as potential influences in a receiver's motivation, an individual's involvement and need for cognition are two that consistently appear as predictors.

Individuals are high in involvement of an issue when they believe that the issue is personally relevant to their lives. Voters who find either politics or a particular political issue to be very relevant to their lives will have a higher level of involvement. For example, active military personnel will find military issues to be relevant to their lives and, therefore, have a higher level of involvement in, and potential to process, political messages related to military issues. Similarly, families that include, or business owners who employ, immigrants will possess higher levels of involvement in political issues related to immigration reform, and consequently be more likely to possess the motivation to elaborate related arguments.

For individuals with high levels of involvement, strong argument quality is important and exerts a significant impact on attitudes (Petty, Cacioppo & Goldman, 1981). For individuals with low levels of involvement, argument quality is less important, but the perceived expertise of the source is important. Similarly, individuals' need for cognition influences their motivation to elaborate on persuasive messages. Need for cognition is a basic personality trait that reflects how much a person enjoys "effortful cognitive activity" (Cacioppo, Petty, Feinstein & Jarvis, 1996, p. 198). It reflects individuals' desires and needs to understand situations and, as a result, is a factor that influences their motivation to elaborate on persuasive arguments. Need for cognition is a personality trait, and although related in that you must have a certain degree of intelligence to be capable of processing information, it is not the same as intelligence level. An individual can possess a high level of intelligence, yet not enjoy thinking about things. When individuals are high in need for cognition, they want to think about the messages they encounter, making them motivated to pay attention, recall the arguments, seek out further information, and generate their own issue-related considerations (Cacioppo et al., 1996). All of which is indicative of using the central processing route.

In contrast, those with a lower need for cognition lack the desire to engage in a more thoughtful processing and seek a simpler path to attitude formation. They rely on simple (peripheral) cues to guide them in processing persuasive message.

FACTORS INFLUENCING ELABORATION AND ROUTE: ABILITY

The second predictor of route to persuasion is ability. Receivers' ability to engage in issue-related thinking, and, subsequently, process persuasive information using the central route, is impacted by distraction and prior knowledge (O'Keefe, 2002). If an individual is distracted by a stimulus, either external or internal, during the reception of a persuasive message, the ability to formulate issue-related thoughts decreases. Whereas distraction decreases the ability to use the central route, prior knowledge about the topic increases a receiver's ability. The more extensive a receiver's prior knowledge is on the persuasive topic, the more likely and able to engage in greater issue-related thinking, subsequently reducing the need to rely on peripheral cues for decision-making (Cacioppo, Petty & Sidera, 1982). High prior knowledge will provide a solid base for processing information through the central route.

HIGH ELABORATION: ELABORATION VALENCE

For individuals under high elaboration conditions, the success of persuasive messages will largely depend on the outcome, positive or negative, of their thoughtful consideration of the message content. This positive or negative assessment of the message and related issue-relevant thoughts is the elaboration valence. When a receiver has both the motivation and ability to process a message through the central route, the success of that persuasive message depends on this elaboration valence of the receiver. If the receiver has positive or favorable thoughts about the message, it will be successful in creating attitude change in its intended direction. However, if the receiver processes the message through the central route and has negative or unfavorable thoughts about the message, attitude change will not be successful as intended by the message. Elaboration valence is impacted by the strength or quality of the message's arguments and whether the message's supported position is proattitudinal or counterattitudinal.

INFLUENCES ON ELABORATION VALENCE

The valence of elaboration is impacted by receivers' initial attitude about the supported position. When the message is proattitudinal, or supports a position already deemed favorable by the receiver, the receiver will be more likely to have favorable thoughts about the message and its advocated position. Similarly, when the message is counterattitudinal, or supports a position already deemed unfavorable by the receiver, the receiver will have unfavorable thoughts about the message. Therefore, in most situations, persuaders can expect proattitudinal messages to induce favorable elaborations and counterattitudinal messages to induce unfavorable elaborations.

However, sometimes people are persuaded by counterattitudinal messages. If not, no one would ever change their mind or be persuaded. The strength of a message's arguments is a determining factor in the success of counterattitudinal messages. When individuals are processing through the central route, using high elaboration to form thoughts, they are both motivated and able to process issue-related thoughts after carefully attending to the message. Therefore, for people thoughtfully examining a message's arguments, the quality or strength of the arguments will also impact the elaboration valence (Petty, Cacioppo & Schumann, 1983).

LOW ELABORATION: HEURISTICS

For individuals under low levels of elaboration, who will not be carefully and thoughtfully considering the content of persuasive messages due to low motivation and/or ability, the success of persuasive messages will often depend on other factors, primarily credibility, liking, and consensus. Individuals rely on heuristic principles when desiring or needing to make decisions requiring little information processing. These heuristics are triggered by peripheral cues, or extrinsic conditions of the message or speaker. For example, individuals with low involvement may agree with a persuasive message simply because they find the source to be credible, invoking the heuristic "If it is from a credible source, I'll agree." This particular heuristic can be triggered by many peripheral cues. For example, an individual might believe a "Dr." to be a credible source on health-related information, or someone with "experience" in politics to be a viable candidate, or even such visual cues as "age" or "wearing glasses" as looking the part of being credible. For those low involvement individuals, any of those peripherals would trigger the heuristic of credibility when faced with a persuasive argument. In commercial marketing, toothpaste brands may use dentist credibility to sell their toothpaste, or pain relievers may use the credibility inferred by doctors to sell their medicine, and athletic brands will use famous athletes to establish credibility with audiences to sell shoes and clothing. In political campaigns, candidates will demonstrate their credibility by focusing on previous experience or office held.

Credibility would not be nearly as impactful of a factor for individuals with high involvement, as supported by research demonstrating a decrease in communicator credibility effects with higher levels of personal relevance (Byrne, Guillory, Mathios, Avery & Hart, 2012; Petty, Cacioppo & Goldman, 1981). However, for those less involved due to low motivation (from low personal involvement or other mentioned factors) or ability, credibility can be a persuasive heuristic cue.

Similarly, a second heuristic is liking. For individuals with low involvement, how much the receiver likes the communicator can impact the persuasiveness of the message. Liked communicators have a persuasive advantage over disliked communicators. The "liking" heuristic can be triggered by a variety of peripheral cues, such as appearance, humor, background, similarity, and so on, "I like the source; therefore, I'll agree with the message." As with credibility, the more a receiver elaborates a message, the less liking impacts overall persuasiveness of the message. In commercial marketing, a makeup manufacturer may use a movie star as model because audience "like" her or they may use a beautiful model because people "like" attractive people. In political campaigning, candidates try to create liking by doing things such as establishing a similarity with voters (e.g., "He's just like me, and I like me.") or giving voters a reason to like them (e.g., "He's such a family man, and I like that.").

The third main heuristic is consensus, which is similar to a "bandwagon" concept in persuasion. The more people support a persuasive argument, the more credence individuals with low involvement will give that message, and the more likely they are to agree with it themselves. For example, the heuristic "if enough people think this, it must be true" would be activated by peripheral cues such as overhearing a group of people talking, reading editorials in support of an issue, or seeing a crowd of people at an event. This technique is used in commercial advertising by demonstrating a demand for a product. "If all of those people want it, I should too!" Similarly, word-of-mouth advertising depends on consensus. "If I hear all of these people talking about a service, it must be something I want/need." In political campaigning, candidates use crowds of people to demonstrate their level of support, initiating the heuristic, "in enough people support this candidate, she must be a good one."

As with credibility, as motivation and ability increase (through personal relevance, prior knowledge, need for cognition, etc.) and involvement increases, the impact of the liking and consensus heuristics decreases.

ROLE OF ELM IN POLITICAL DECISION-MAKING: LITERATURE REVIEW

As a model of persuasion that addresses the message processing and persuasion, the ELM is highly applicable to political communication, yet remarkably under-researched. Petty and Cacioppo (1986) looked specifically at need for cognition, finding a direct relationship between high political knowledge and high need for cognition. Additionally, the researchers found the preelection attitudes of high need for cognition voters to be better predictors of voting behavior than that of low need for cognition voters. This attitude-behavior consistency for high need for cognition individuals was indicative of high involvement elaboration via the central route (Petty & Cacioppo, 1986). However, even within the limited research in this area, results are conflicting.

Kam (2005) also addressed need for cognition. However, she found that, rather than need for cognition, it is political awareness that predicts elaboration and, subsequently, which route voters will take when making voting decisions. Less politically aware individuals use political party as a peripheral cue. Kam found that, as political awareness increased, reliance on political party as a cue decreased, and voters elaborated more as they used the central route for processing political information. Political awareness as a factor is consistent with higher prior knowledge as a factor for high elaboration.

Mondak (1990) looked at the various functions source credibility can play in political decision-making. The role of source credibility is dependent upon the effort expended the process the message through either central processing or peripheral cues. Individuals who are engaging in low elaboration may use credibility as a heuristic; this is especially relevant in political decision-making, when the quantity and complexity of information is high (Mondak, 1990). Rather than considering the details of the message, individuals can use credibility as a peripheral cue to form their thoughts guided by their credibility heuristic (i.e., "If the source is credible, I agree.") Individuals engaging in high elaboration may also use credibility, but instead of using it as a peripheral cue, they would use it as persuasive evidence included in their thought processing (Mondak, 1990). For both high and low involvement conditions, credibility has an effect on message evaluation.

Chmielewski (2012) found consistent results over three election cycles, with predictor variables of voting behavior to be different, depending on level of elaboration. Candidate image and favorability were predictive of voting behavior under high elaboration via the central route, while favorability, credibility, image, and political party affiliation were predictive of voting behavior under low involvement processing (Chmielewski, 2012). Like credibility in Mondak's (1990) research, favorability serves both high and low involvement in different ways, both as a peripheral cue guiding a heuristic and as persuasive evidence. In Chmielewski's research, however, consistent with ELM research, credibility served only as a predictor in low involvement processing. Political party affiliation was also a peripheral cue, triggering a heuristic rule (e.g., "I vote Republican. The candidate is a Republican, so I will vote for him.").

ROLE OF ELM IN POLITICAL DECISION-MAKING: HIGH ELABORATION AND CENTRAL PROCESSING

Although existing research in this particular area is limited, it supports the applicability of ELM for political communication, both for high and low elaboration processing. The two factors influencing individuals' motivation are involvement and need for cognition. Involvement, in a political environment, would include political involvement, political participation (i.e., political discussion and curiosity), and political interest. The politically involved and interested are more likely to seek political information (Tan, 1980) and to use it more purposefully (Chaffee & Schleuder, 1986; Pinkleton & Austin, 1998). Political participation predicts message attention to both proattitudinal and counterattitudinal messages (Chaffee, Saphir, Graf, Sandvig & Hahn, 2001), and individuals who are more politically involved are the most open to the opposition of counterattitudinal messages and allow exposure and attention to the message (Chaffee et al., 2001).

Relatedly, the two factors influencing ability are prior knowledge and distraction. In a political environment, prior knowledge would be relevant to include prior political knowledge. The meaning and significance of new political information depend on the amount of political knowledge that a person brings to the new information (Price & Zaller, 1993). The more extensive individuals' background knowledge is regarding the political issue, the more able they will be to process new message content.

Therefore, applying an ELM framework to a political environment, individuals attending to politically related information to make political decisions will possess the critical factors of high elaboration and use the central route for processing political information, provided that their motivation (i.e., involvement, participation, interest, discussion, and curiosity, as well as need for cognition) and ability (i.e., prior political knowledge, as well as limited distraction) are high. However, with all of the content and complexities related to political content, the internal and external distractions individuals face, and a basic predisposition of some to possess a low need for cognition, when faced with processing political information, many will process through low elaboration, instead relying on peripheral cues to trigger existing heuristic rules.

ROLE OF ELM IN POLITICAL DECISION-MAKING: LOW ELABORATION AND HEURISTIC CUES

For individuals under low levels of elaboration facing political information, the success of politically related persuasive messages will often depend on factors such as credibility, liking, and consensus, which are highly relevant to a political environment. While credibility is a source effect, it is a receiver-based construct in that credibility is bestowed upon the source by the receiver. Credibility is a judgment call, by the message receiver, as to the believability of the source. Receivers determine a source's credibility based on a variety of dimensions: expertise (competence and knowledge), trustworthiness (character), goodwill (perceived caring), dynamism or extroversion, and composure. Overall, high credibility speakers are more effective and persuasive than low credibility speakers. In a political environment, audience perception of the credibility of political candidates, political and organizational leaders, and all aspects of the media is continuously influx. Each of those groups is constantly trying to demonstrate their expertise, trustworthiness, and goodwill through speeches, advertisements, appearances, and other accolades. Additionally, the public expects a certain degree of dynamism and composure from political and media figures. Audiences draw on all of these aspects when perceiving how credible a political or media source is. While, as suggested by Mondak's (1990) research, this may factor into high elaboration processing of persuasive argument quality, per the ELM, for low elaboration individuals, this credibility would serve as a peripheral cue, triggering the heuristic rule "If I find the source credible, I will agree with the message."

Similarly, liked sources are much more persuasive, especially for low elaboration individuals. In general, liking is positively related to similarity, even if it's only a perception of similarity, physical attractiveness, social exchange, and reinforcement. Individuals like people who they deem to be similar to them, as that similarity provides reinforcement, reassurance, and comfort. Whether faced with others who demonstrate similar behavior, attitudes, beliefs, values, abilities, or personality from another, individuals find that positively rewarding and determine that they like those others. Knowing this, political figures craft their image to include a degree of "liking," as they recognize how important it is for voters and audiences to "like" them. They work to demonstrate their similarity, whether politically relevant or not, in behavior (e.g., "I spend time with my family too."), attitude (e.g., "I have a favorable attitude toward gun control too."), beliefs (e.g., "I believe education is important too."), values (e.g., "God is at the forefront on my life and thoughts too."), abilities (e.g., "I play golf too."), or personality (e.g., "I am honest too.") with audiences/voters, knowing that if they feel a sense of similarity, they will like them. For high involvement audiences, liking may only be a small facet on which they base their evaluations, but for low involvement voters, liking is a significant peripheral cue on which they process messages, triggering the heuristic "If I like you, I will agree with your message," which is the heuristic which, especially for political candidates, is important and can garner critical votes.

The third main heuristic is consensus, which is depicted in the political environment by political figures and through media outlets. Whether it's through the visual portrayals of a candidate or cause's supporters, or via endorsements by other political figures, media outlets or celebrities, the depiction demonstrates to audiences that others are giving them their support. Humans are social beings and they often will follow the crowd, especially when under low elaboration conditions. Seeing that others support the candidate, leader, or cause can be the peripheral cue that triggers the heuristic, "If others support, I will too."

CELEBRITY AS A HEURISTIC

Per the ELM, for low elaboration individuals, credibility, liking, and consensus are the main heuristics. Credibility is partially based on dynamism and extroversion, and a related facet of credibility refers to an indefinable charm or allure—charisma. Liking is partially based on physical attractiveness, and a facet of consensus is demonstrated through endorsement by others. Celebrities fit all of these. They're charismatic and dynamic. Celebrities are physically attractive, and people like attractive people. Celebrities are liked, if not only for their appearance, for their music or movies or talents. When a political figure or cause can gain celebrity endorsements, it demonstrates that others, namely attractive people who we like and deem credible, support them or their cause, it merges credibility, liking, and consensus, a trifecta in peripheral cues, making celebrity itself a potential heuristic for low involvement elaboration and message processing.

Both endorsements and branding use the celebrity's brand as a heuristic cue to raise the salience of a candidate or issue in the audience's mind. Politics is a world of social networks, and celebrities can bring political causes and candidates their large networks, as well as the money and media attention that follows. A celebrity makes a particular candidate or cause stand out and it serves as a peripheral cue. As a white female, I may not have paid as much attention to Black Lives Matter without my connection to LeBron James—I'm from Cleveland and have watched him closely since he was in high school (I have a LeBron bobblehead in my office). When he started speaking up for BLM, LeBron himself served as the peripheral cue to trigger the heuristic, "I like LeBron James, and he's active in Black Lives Matter, so I pay attention to that movement." When he was told to "shut up and dribble," it made me feel angry on LeBron's behalf because of my positive feelings toward him. Similarly, I like Reese Witherspoon. She's a talented actress. I like her movies. She seems highly likeable—she's attractive, and I have the perception that we'd be similar—successful woman, same age, blonde, has young children, dresses attractively, lives in the South. If she lived in my neighborhood, I'm certain we'd be friends. This liking and perception of similarity have allowed her to be a peripheral cue for me to purchase clothing from her label *Draper James*. Now, I know that she profits directly from my purchases, so when she is cultivating her brand, creating the likeable, adorable, "I'm just like you" image that I have bought into, I know it is profitable for her. If I am willing to purchase clothing from her, supporting her commercial ventures, then when it's a cause she believes in, yet, personally doesn't profit from, I would definitely show support. Reese Witherspoon's celebrity status would be the peripheral cue that triggers the heuristic "I like and support Reese Witherspoon, and she's active in the Time's Up movement, so I agree with that movement." As a woman, I would possibly be a more high involvement processor of a cause related to women's issue. In that case, Reese Witherspoon's celebrity would also serve as evidence for me in addition to serving as a peripheral cue for more low involvement processors. As discussed in chapter 1, these celebrities' brands transfer to their causes, candidates, and commercial ventures. In chapter 3 we'll touch on receiver effects, to look at the effects of our parasocial relationships with celebrities, as well as how we think other receivers will be affected by the celebrity heuristic through third-person effects.

REFERENCES

Byrne, S., Guillory, J. E., Mathios, A., Avery, R., & Hart, S. (2012). The unintended consequences of disclosure: The impact of manipulating sponsor identification on the perceived credibility and effectiveness of smoking cessation. *Journal of Health Communication, 17*, 1119–1137.

Cacioppo, J. R., Petty, R. E., Feinstein, J. A., & Jarvis, W. B. G. (1996). Dispositional differences in cognitive motivation: The life and times of individuals varying in need for cognition. *Psychological Bulletin, 119*, 197–253.

Cacioppo, J. T., Petty, R. E., & Sidera, J. A. (1982). The effects of a salient self-schema on the evaluation of proattitudinal editorials: Top-down versus bottom-up message processing. *Journal of Experimental Psychology, 18*(4), 324–338.

Chaffee, S. H., Saphir, M. N., Graf, J., Sandvig, C., & Hahn, K. S. (2001). Attention to counter-attitudinal messages in a state election campaign. *Political Communication, 18*, 247–272.

Chaffee, S. H., & Schleuder, J. (1986). Measurement and effects of attention to media news. *Human Communication Research, 13*, 373–399.

Chmielewski, T. (2012). Applying the elaboration likelihood model to voting. *The International Journal of Interdisciplinary Social Science, 6*(10), 33–47.

Kam, C. D. (2005). Who toes the party line? Cues, values, and individual differences. *Political Behavior, 27*(2), 163–182.

Mondak, J. J. (1990). Perceived legitimacy of Supreme Court decisions: Three functions of source credibility. *Political Behavior, 12*(4), 363–384.

O'Keefe, D. (2002). *Persuasion: Theory and Research.* Thousand Oaks, CA: Sage.

Open Secrets Center for Responsive Politics. (2017). *2016 Election.* Retrieved July 18, 2018 from http://www.opensecrets.org.

Petty, R. E., & Cacioppo, J. T. (1983). The role of bodily responses in attitude measurement and change. In J. T. Caceoppo, & R. E. Petty (Eds.), *Social Psychphysiology: A Sourcebook,* 51–101. New York, NY: Guilford Press.

Petty, R. E., & Cacioppo, J. T. (1986). The elaboration likelihood model of persuasion. In L. Berkowitz (Ed.), *Advances in Experimental Social Psychology*, 123–205. New York, NY: Academic Press.

Petty, R. E., Cacioppo, J. T., & Goldman, R. (1981). Personal involvement as a determinant of argument-based persuasion. *Journal of Personality and Social Psychology, 41*, 847–855.

Petty, R. E., Cacioppo, J. T., & Schumann, D. (1983). Central and peripheral routes to advertising effectiveness: The moderating role of involvement. *Journal of Consumer Research, 10*(2), 135–146.

Chapter 3

Persuasion
Receiver Effects

In chapter 2, we looked at the source—what is it about a message's source that may impact our reception of a persuasive message? Whether low involvement or high involvement, a celebrity's "celebrity" provides them a degree of influence, either as a peripheral cue or evidence. But receivers play a part in this process too. In this chapter, we look at the receiver side of the persuasive effect. How does the receiver perceive the message because of the source? We'll focus on two persuasion concepts critical to understanding why celebrities can exert a persuasive influence over us and others: parasocial interaction and third-person effects.

Let's return to LeBron James. When LeBron left the Cleveland Cavaliers in 2010 for Miami, and now again in 2018 for LA, fans weren't just upset to lose a superstar—they felt betrayed by a friend—a real friend. When teaching receiver effects in my persuasion classes, I often use LBJ as an example, joking how if we met, we'd totally be friends. I, like many others, have watched him grow up, from the high school player at St. Vincent-St. Mary in Akron, through the ups and downs of leaving Cleveland, returning, and winning a championship. We admire his loyalty to his high school sweetheart wife and his adorable children. We appreciate all he's done for Cleveland—our town—his and ours (well, until I left over a dozen years ago, which somehow was OK for me to leave, but not him). We call him "LeBron" because that's how you refer to friends, by first name. We talk about him and his decisions, just as we talk about our other friends. When rumors were circulating about if he'd leave Cleveland, we talked about it as if he actually was our friend, saying things like "he wants a good place to raise his family." How would we know what he wants for his family? It's not as if we had coffee last week and discussed it. As much as I'd like to think we're tight, I don't actually know him, and he certainly doesn't know me, and while I (reluctantly) recognize this as purely a fan-celebrity relationship, some don't.

PARASOCIAL INTERACTION

For certain media consumers, media and its personalities are more than just entertainment. Audiences often form a type of friendship or "pseudofriendship" with the characters they watch day after day or week after week. Horton and Wohl (1956) defined parasocial interaction as a one-sided relationship or intimate friendship between a media consumer and a radio or television persona. The researchers continued that this one-sided relationship is also "nondialectical, controlled by the performer, and not susceptible of mutual development" (p. 215). Parasocial relationships include elements of involvement, intimacy, and even friendship. The bond within these pseudofriendships contains empathy, physical and social attraction, perceived similarity, shared values, attitudes, background, and similarity in communicative style (Cohen, 1997; Kim & Rubin, 1997). However, these apparent face-to-face relationships between media characters and audience members are imaginary and out of the audience's control. It is only an illusion of intimacy, yet, oftentimes, the viewer fails to acknowledge the nonreciprocal nature of the relationship.

Parasocial relationships may be experienced and understood differently for different people. For some, these pseudofriendships may be intimate and serve their attachment needs. For others, they may be friendships, idolization, or various other forms of relationship (Cohen, 1997). Interaction with media can range on a continuum from detachment to fanaticism. Admirers often think and speak of celebrities as if there were a relationship between them. They come to know these psuedofriends as they do the people they encounter in their daily lives: through description, prediction, and explanation. Audiences make observations about media persona, from inferences about their attitudes and behaviors, and even develop attributions or explanations for their behavior (Rubin & Rubin, 2001).

Audience members participate mentally in media characters' lives. Viewers feel comfortable with the media persona, as they do with a friend. They feel that the media personality is down-to-earth and natural—someone they would choose to be friends with—and they empathize with and look forward to seeing or listening to them on a regular basis.

Parasocial Relationships and Interpersonal Relationships

Viewers refer to feelings and heuristics developed from their real-life experiences when using media (Rubin & Rubin, 1985). They judge celebrities as they do the people in their own lives. Viewers use the same criteria to evaluate both media figures and people they encounter in person. In many ways, parasocial relationships are similar to interpersonal relationships, and the formation of these pseudofriendships relates to the viewers' socially learned expectations about interpersonal interactions (Rubin, Perse & Powell, 1985). Audiences apply what they have experienced in their interpersonal relationships and use that knowledge in the development of relationships with characters to which they are frequently exposed. Parasocial interaction is based on the same principles as interpersonal relationships: attraction, perceived similarity, length of acquaintance, uncertainty reduction, and attribution.

Parasocial relationships follow a similar developmental process as in the formation of interpersonal relationships. This development process is related to the amount of exposure to the persona, the liking of, and attraction to, the media character. As with interpersonal relationships, those who are perceived to be real and similar to us are the characters with whom viewers form an active bond (Rubin et al., 1985). Social attraction is important in the parasocial interaction process (Rubin & McHugh, 1987). When celebrities are socially attractive and create a context for interaction, audiences develop a relationship with them.

In both social and parasocial relationships, the longer the relationship, the stronger the relationship (Perse & Rubin, 1989). The more interaction that occurs, the more likely it is that a relationship will develop between the viewer and the media persona. Over time, audiences begin to feel that they know media persona as they know their own friends and, therefore, they are able to predict their behavior. The exposure to, and regularity of, celebrities in our lives today, from their performances to media coverage to following them on social media, lead to the formation of parasocial relationships. Relationship importance is increased in both interpersonal and parasocial relationships through repeated exposure and attraction.

Regular interaction with media persona serves to reduce the uncertainty viewers initially feel, and allows for the parasocial relationship to develop. Liking, exposure, communication, and intimacy are major components in the uncertainty reduction and relationship development processes of both interpersonal and parasocial relationships. Each interaction with the media persona helps the viewer to form an opinion about them, which they carry into the next parasocial event (Auter, 1992). As with interpersonal relationship formation, each interaction builds on the last.

Rubin and Rubin (2001) suggested that with the formation of parasocial pseudofriendships comes the feeling that the viewer can make attributions about the actions of the media characters. The researchers explained attribution theory as a way for individuals to understand why actions occur by attributing them either to the circumstances or to personality or dispositional elements. Attributions are used to predict or explain behavior. Over time, as uncertainty is reduced, viewers feel an intimate bond with media persona and a parasocial relationship is formed.

In today's highly mediated environment, in addition to consuming the celebrities' tangible products (e.g., watching their movies, their TV shows, or their games and listening to their music), we read about them in magazines and online, we see them or stories about them on entertainment news shows and we follow them on social media. We see them in so many different ways, that we feel like we know them. We are mentally participating in their lives, and we think and speak as if we actually are. As we discussed in chapter 1, the celebrities have often crafted their brand to depict them as down-to-earth or natural—just like us. "Celebrities . . . they're just like us." We can imagine being friends with them, and our friends are persuasive. We listen when our friends recommend a restaurant, a movie, or a book. When our friends believe in a cause, we too believe in it, or at least pay attention to it, because we find our friends to be socially attractive, similar to us, and we've known them for long enough to trust their judgment, which is why the parallels between interpersonal and parasocial relationships are critical to understanding why celebrities can have an effect on the receiver. If our friends can be persuasive, so can our pseudo friends.

THIRD-PERSON EFFECTS

OK, so I may, as I mentioned in chapter 2, like Reese Witherspoon, and it may even be enough to lead me to go see her movies and order her clothes, but just because I like her, I am a smart receiver. I realize that she is selling her brand, and her movies, and her clothing line, and even her support of political candidates and causes. I am not going to support an entire social movement or vote for a political candidate simply because she endorses the cause or the candidate. Don't worry—I don't think that you're going to be influenced into taking a stance or casting a vote simply because Reese tells you to. I know, like me, you're too informed for that. But you know who will support a cause or vote for a candidate simply because Reese Witherspoon tells them to? Them. Not me, and not you, but they will—the third person.

Davison (1983) proposed the third-person effect hypothesis based on anecdotal sociological evidence, and research substantiated the claim. Third-person effect predicts that people will overestimate the persuasive power of mass media messages on the attitudes and behaviors of others. The belief is that, whereas persuasive communication will not affect "you" or "me," it will affect "them," the third person. People evaluate the likely effect of persuasive media messages and compare their own reaction with that of others both in and beyond their reference groups (Tewksbury, Moy, & Weis, 2004).

Anecdotal examples and empirical scholarly research consistently support a third-person effect. For example, Davison (1983) attributed fluctuations in the stock market to third-person effect. The fluctuations are often credited to rumors or news reports. People anticipate that the reports will cause others to either buy or sell stocks; therefore, they buy or sell to anticipate others' actions.

Salwen (1998) found a similar third-person effect in election censorship research. He determined that people perceived election campaign messages to have a greater influence on others than on themselves. Based on this perception, they supported the censorship and restriction of election messages. Accordingly, Perloff (1996) reported that fifteen of sixteen studies examined supported the perceptual hypothesis. Both Paxton (1995) and Tiedge, Silverbatt, Havice, and Rosenfeld (1991) reported that more than 90 percent of respondents perceived greater media effects on others than on themselves. Lo and Wei (2002) determined that a third-person effect exists with internet pornography. The researchers reported that people believe that internet pornography has a greater negative impact on others than on themselves. Women perceived the negative effects to be greater on other males than on other females. This effect supports the third-person hypothesis' idea of the impact of social distance.

Social distance is a key variable in third person's supposition that perceived effects are greater for the third person than for "me" or "you" (Meirick, 2004). The greater the social distance between a person and a group, the greater the gap in the perceived impact of a persuasive message (Meirick, 2004). For example, residents in Wilmington, North Carolina, would believe that a negative news story would have a small impact on "self," a larger impact on "other Wilmingtonians," an even larger impact on "other North Carolinians," and the largest impact on the "public opinion at large." Similarly, Meirick (2004) discussed perceived effects on "in-groups," or self, versus "out-groups," or them. People make group comparisons; they highlight the similarities to in-group members and the differences with out-group members. This reference group approach to social distance is relevant in political contexts. For example, Republicans viewing an anti-Republican ad would see the smallest effect on themselves, a larger effect on other Republicans, the in-group, and the largest effect on Democrats, the out-group. When addressing the effects of political advertising on reference groups, Meirick found a greater perceived effect of the out-group candidate's ads on the out-group and general public than on self or in-group.

Although third-person effects have been clearly documented in over twenty years of empirical research, the hypothesis is often criticized because scholars still lack a clear understanding of a cause for this phenomenon—why people perceive themselves to be smarter and less affected by media messages than others (Paul, Salwen, & Dupagne, 2000; Price, Huang, & Tewksbury, 1997). There are, however, a number of possible explanations as to why this third-person effect occurs. First, people believe that they have information unavailable to other people. Because "they" don't know what "we" know, they are more likely to be influenced by the persuasive media message. Second, people with each point of view see the media as biased against their side; therefore, they assume a disproportionate effect will occur because of the arguments or facts supporting the "wrong" side of the issue. People believe that, in order to have a balanced media, the coverage would need to be skewed toward the "correct" side of the issue. Because it's merely a statement of the obvious truth, they don't see the correct side of the issue as being persuasive. Third, Meirick (2004) explained third-person effects as occurring due to self-enhancement. When a persuasive media message is seen as undesirable, a third-person effect occurs. However, if a message is seen to be desirable, or that it would be smart for a person to be influenced by it, third-person effect is minimized. Fourth, Salwen (1998) suggested that people have limited understanding of their thoughts and cognitive processes. They believe that they are much more discerning about harmful media messages than they really are. Therefore, they believe that they are unaffected by the negative messages when they actually are affected. Others, however, believe to be less discerning and, therefore, vulnerable to the powerful media.

Critics also suggest that third-person effects research has failed "to identify the contingent factors that might enhance or diminish the perception" (Paul et al., 2000, p. 58). Mason (1995) even proposed that the third-person effect is "a phenomenon without a clear process explanation" (p. 612). Similarly, research has also failed to adequately explain what causes some individuals to be resilient to these persuasive messages (Paul et al., 2000). For example, according to Lasorsa (1992), 50 percent of a sample is susceptible to the effect and 50 percent is not. Research fails to thoroughly explain either side. However, while relevant, this criticism of the process does not negate the need to address its application into our current political structure.

Third-Person Effects and Politics

With the increasingly blurred line between Hollywood and Washington and the support of Hollywood's biggest celebrities, it is important to address the effects these endorsements have on the voters. Individuals often believe that they are not as susceptible to persuasive messages as the general public. They feel that they have information unavailable to other people; others are susceptible because "they" don't know what "we" know. In elections filled with political polarization, when people are very strong in their political convictions and often unwavering in support of their presidential candidate and overall, political parties hold their bases, a celebrity endorsement supporting a candidate will not have any room to influence voters' decisions because they are already in favor of the endorsed candidate (Brubaker, 2011). However, voters do believe that others have the potential to be persuaded by the opposing candidate's endorsements (Brubaker, 2011). See appendix A for a further case study of the role of third-person effects and celebrity endorsements in the 2004, 2008, and 2012 presidential elections.

Very little research has been conducted to determine the effects of celebrity endorsements on politics (Garthwaite & Moore, 2008). Endorsements, in general, represent an area with little research, primarily due to the lack of an appropriate measure to determine the endorsement's impact (Stratmann, 2005). In the 2008 presidential election campaign, a Pew Research study (2007) found that 15 percent of voters said they would be more likely to vote for a political candidate endorsed by Oprah Winfrey (Obama). While 69 percent of respondents said that their vote would be unaffected by the endorsement, 60 percent said that they believed the endorsement would help Obama, demonstrating a third-person effect for Oprah's endorsement (Pew, 2007). Garthwaite and Moore (2007) also found strong evidence that Oprah's endorsement of Obama during the 2008 Democratic primary had an impact on both Obama's success and the overall voter turnout. The researchers estimated that Oprah's endorsement was responsible for 1,015,559 votes for Obama, in an election where Obama defeated Hillary Clinton by only 278,966 votes, and that Oprah's endorsement was responsible for increasing voter turnout by 2,196,476—a substantial amount in an election where 33,386,184 votes were cast. In addition, evidence suggests that celebrities have the ability to influence fans' behavior in many areas, such as product endorsements. Therefore, it is logical to assume that if fans can be influenced to purchase a product due to a celebrity's paid support then these endorsements should also be effective in the political realm where there is no direct financial incentive to the celebrity endorser (Garthwaite & Moore, 2008).

If George Clooney is deemed influential enough to be paid to sell Omega watches and Oprah Winfrey can increase sales of a 130-year-old novel, *Anna Karenina*, 5,421 percent simply by choosing it as an Oprah Book Club book, it's logical to assume that these celebrities would have a similar impact on the political world. However, with only 15 percent admitting that they would be positively influenced by Oprah's endorsement of a political candidate and 60 percent believing that her endorsement would benefit a candidate, a discrepancy clearly exists. It is important for political communication research to continue to examine this discrepancy as well as the greater impact of the endorsement. In chapter 5 we'll look at next presidential election, the highly celebritized 2016 election, and in chapter 6, the ensuing climate of ever-increasing celebrity activism that has followed.

REFERENCES

Auter, P. J. (1992). TV that talks back: An experimental validation of the Parasocial Interaction Scale. *Journal of Broadcasting & Electronic Media, 36*, 173–181.

Brubaker, J. (2011). It doesn't affect my vote: Third-person effects of celebrity endorsements on college voters in the 2004 and 2008 presidential elections. *American Communication Journal, 13*(2), 4–22.

Cohen, J. (1997). Parasocial relations and romantic attraction: Gender and dating status differences. *Journal of Broadcasting & Electronic Media, 41*, 516–530.

Davison, W. P. (1983). The third-person effect in communication. *Public Opinion Quarterly, 47*, 1–15.

Horton, D., & Wohl, R. R. (1956). Mass communication and para-social interaction: Observations on intimacy at a distance. *Psychiatry, 19*, 215–229.

Kim, J. K., & Rubin, A. M. (1997). The variable influence of audience activity on media effects. *Communication Research, 24*, 107–135.

Lasorsa, D. L. (1992). How media affect policymakers: The third-person effect. In J. D. Kennamer (Ed.), *Public Opinion, the Press and Public Policy* (pp. 163–175). New York, NY: Praeger.

Lo, V., & Wei, R. (2002). Third-person effect, gender, and pornography on the internet. *Journal of Broadcasting & Electronic Media, 46*, 13–33.

Mason, L. (1995). Newspaper as repeater: An experiment on defamation and the third-person effect. *Journalism & Mass Communication Quarterly, 72*, 610–620.

Media Vest USA. (2004, September 30). *Word to Presidential Hopefuls: Celebrities on Campaign Trail Reach Young Voters.* Retrieved March 22, 2005 from http://www.mediaweek.com.

Meirick, P. C. (2004). Topic-relevant reference groups and dimensions of distance: Political advertising and first- and third-person effects. *Communication Research, 31*, 234–255.

Paul, B., Salwen, M. B., & Dupagne, M. (2000). The third-person effect: A meta-analysis of the perceptual hypothesis. *Mass Communication & Society, 3*, 57–85.

Paxton, M. A. (1995). The third-person effect and attitudes toward freedom of expression. *Dissertation Abstracts International, 57*(2), 498A.

Perloff, R. M. (1996). Perceptions and conceptions of political media impact: The third-person effect and beyond. In A. N. Crigler (Ed.), *The Psychology of Political Communication* (pp. 177–191). Ann Arbor, MI: University of Michigan Press.

Perse, E. M., & Rubin, R. B. (1989). Attribution in social and parasocial relationships. *Communication Research, 16*, 59–77.

Pew Research Center. (2007, September 20). *The Oprah Factor and Campaign 2008: Do Political Endorsements Matter?* Retrieved May 25, 2009 from http://people-press.org/report/357/the-oprah-factor-and-campaign-2008.

Price, V., Huang, L., & Tewksbury, D. (1997). Third-person effects of news coverage: Orientations toward media. *Journalism & Mass Communication Quarterly, 74*, 525–540.

Rubin, A. M., Perse, E. M., & Powell, R. A. (1985). Loneliness, parasocial interaction, and local television news viewing. *Human Communication Research, 12*, 155–180.

Rubin, A. M., & Rubin, R. B. (1985). Interface of personal and mediated communication: A research agenda. *Critical Studies in Mass Communication, 2*, 36–53.

Rubin, R. B., & McHugh, M. P. (1987). Development of parasocial interaction relationships. *Journal of Broadcasting & Electronic Media, 31*, 279–292.

Rubin, R. B., & Rubin, A. M. (2001). Attribution in social and parasocial relationships. In V. Manusov, & J. H. Harvey (Eds.), *Attribution, Communication Behavior, and Close Relationships* (pp. 320–337). New York, NY: Cambridge University Press.

Salwen, M. B. (1998). Perceptions of media influence and support for censorship: The third-person effect in the 1996 presidential election. *Communication Research, 25*(3), 259–285.

Tewksbury, D., Moy, P., & Weis, D. S. (2004). Preparations for Y2K: Revisiting the behavioral component of the third-person effect. *Journal of Communication, 54*, 138–155.

Tiedge, J. T., Silverblatt, A., Havice, M. J., & Rosenfeld, R. (1991). Discrepancy between perceived first-person and perceived third-person mass media effects. *Journalism Quarterly, 68*, 141–154.

Wong, V. (2012). *Obama vs Romney Celebrity Endorsements: Why Stars Continue to Shine in Election 2012*. Retrieved March 22, 2014, from http://www.policymic.com/articles.

Part II

Chapter 4

History of Celebrities and Politics

For decades, Hollywood A-listers and Washington Insiders have frequently traveled in the same circles and celebrities have taken to endorsing political candidates. Today, however, "the line between Hollywood and Washington has virtually disappeared" (Cannon, 2003, p. 22). Celebrity endorsements have become necessities for both political causes and political candidates. Similarly, being active in various causes has become the thing to do. Celebrities are "woke." "Whether it's to satisfy one's social conscience or to elicit good PR, celebrity activism is becoming the entertainment industry's unofficial pastime" (Smillie, 1998, p. B1). It has reached the point that it is frowned upon to *not* be political. Celebrities are expected—and even called out if they're not (i.e., Trent Reznor/Taylor Swift, as we'll discuss in chapter 6)—to be politically active. Celebrities may even become "accidental activists" when their action, or inaction, intentionally or inadvertently makes a political statement. As we'll discuss in chapter 5, the 2016 election was highly celebritized, with countless endorsements and celebrity candidates. And post-2016, issues such as Black Lives Matter and #metoo have moved celebrities even more into the political spotlight.

Not just activists, the switch from actor to politician is neither a new nor an unrealistic leap. Hollywood and politics require similar skills: an ability to communicate with large groups of people, a capability to perform, and a knack for navigating the throes of fame and power (Grier & McLaughlin, 2003). Former president and actor Ronald Reagan successfully made the switch from actor to governor of California to president of the United States. Arnold Schwarzenegger, former bodybuilder and action star, served two terms as governor of California before returning to Hollywood as a cartoon character called "the Governator," a name he was referred to during his political tenure due to the fame of his role in *The Terminator*. Sonny Bono, child-star

Shirley Temple Black, Ben Jones ("Cooter" from *The Dukes of Hazzard*), and Fred Grandy ("Gopher" from *The Love Boat*) served in Congress. Former pro-wrestler Jesse "The Body" Ventura was elected governor of Minnesota, and Dirty Harry, aka Clint Eastwood, was mayor of Carmel, California. Jerry Springer of daytime fame moved in the other direction, beginning his career as mayor of Cincinnati. Fred Thompson, former star of television's *Law and Order*, moved between the worlds of Hollywood and Washington. Thompson began his career in film, was elected to the senate, returned to television, and, in 2008, made a run for the Republican ticket. It is often the actors' notoriety, developed through their media exposure, that provides the necessary publicity to succeed in full-fledged political careers (Marks & Fischer, 2002). The 2016 election of Donald Trump as president bypassed Hollywood completely, demonstrating that in today's society, celebrity fame supersedes Hollywood pedigree.

Celebrities initially became attached to the Democratic Party and its causes in the 1930s. Possibly, the privileged status of celebrities provides them with a sense of guilt to embrace causes on the Far Left (Baker, 2007). "The left has had a schizophrenic relationship with celebrity. On one side is condemnation: the attention lavished on celebrities is at best a waste of time; at worst, it's a dangerous distraction from more important issues" (Duncombe, 2007, p. 22). On the other side is adoration, and the politics of the Left are legitimized by our modern-day gods—celebrities (Duncombe, 2007). While we often associate celebrities with the left, the link between Hollywood and the conservative right was strong throughout the second half of the twentieth century. Whichever way they lean, Hollywood's biggest celebrities have become some of the most influential political activists. If a celebrity supports a cause or politician, then the public, the media, and policy-makers will take notice.

In chapter 1 we began to understand how celebrities' brands transfer to the products/candidates/causes that they endorse. In chapters 2 and 3, we discussed persuasion and the effects of celebrity sources on receivers. And in chapters 5 and 6, we'll discuss the current state of celebrity in politics, but is this new? In this chapter, we'll look at the history of the celebrity-politics relationship.

HISTORY OF CELEBRITY AND THE AMERICAN POLITICAL PROCESS

The mingling of celebrities and politics has a long history. Many of our earliest leaders, such as George Washington, Andrew Jackson, and Ulysses Grant, used their military fame (their celebrity, as that was the only "celebrity" at the time) as a catalyst to reach political office. As books and magazines became more accessible, audiences consumed the biographies of both historical figures, such as heroes and saints, and contemporary personalities, such as politicians and military leaders. At the same time, portraits were being produced in larger numbers as technology developed from the lithograph to the photograph. The combination of the biography and the photograph, written and visual media, and the propensity for the audience to be drawn to it as entertainment, depict the early origins of celebrity or pop culture.

Political leaders were the first to recognize and utilize the power and influence of this new trend. Throughout the nineteenth century, politics, its rallies, marches, and clubs, were primary forms of entertainment, and "politicians were the nation's first aristocracy of celebrity" (Grier & McLaughlin, 2003, p. 1). At this time, political leaders were the only people who were famous—they were the celebrities. Napoleon was a brilliant self-promoter and one of the earliest public figures to use every medium available at the time to increase his celebrity status, including having himself depicted on wallpaper. Similarly, Queen Victoria, the "first media monarch," used this development of popular print and visual media to reinvent and promote the role of the monarchy (Plunkett, 2003). Pope Pius IX, who was both the longest-serving pope and a political reformer, is considered to be the first pope of the modern era (1846–1878). He is noted, and still criticized by some, for his interest in amassing papal power. He used written and visual media to capture the attention of the public and promote the First Vatican Council, his foreign policy, including involvement with the United States during the civil war, and the church's growth program. All three political leaders are historically known for their self-promotion and their use of the "new media" of the time to rise to a celebrity status among their followers.

During the first half of the twentieth century, Americans became enthralled with the movies, as film provided a way for audiences to escape reality and dive into a fantasy world. Twenty-five years after the first movie theater opening in 1905, nearly 100 percent of the population went to the movie theater regularly, making it prime for its stars to become high-profile celebrities (Ross, 2011). Celebrity involvement in politics at this time was primarily decorative and ceremonial; the political issues they were involved with (i.e., wars, socialism vs. capitalism, McCarthyism, civil rights) overshadowed the celebrities' participation (Marks & Fischer, 2002).

Films were political before the stars themselves, with an ideological diversity that reflected the ideological diversity of American politics (Ross, 2011).

As the popularity of movies grew, and as its critics reacted to film with threats of censorship, movie producers recognized the industry benefits of aligning with politicians. It was industry needs, not partisan ideology, that drove the relationship. In an effort to be independent, movie producers created the Motion Picture Producers' Association (MPPA) in 1916, with the promise to support any politician, regardless of party, who protected their interests. Politicians also saw the benefits of a relationship, as Hollywood was a place to solicit campaign money. The MPAA required campaign contributions from its members, using the funds to support any candidate, regardless of party identification, who supported their interests.

The relationship between politics and the film industry is robust; political films included a range of biographical films, films about politics, and films as political propaganda. Each was, in its own way, a contribution to the realm of visual politics. It wasn't long before the celebrities themselves became political activists, with some of these film stars using this new medium to promote their political agenda.

HOLLYWOOD'S LIBERAL TRAMP

One of the most notable celebrity film activists was Charlie Chaplin, who became a public champion for the poor over the rich, labor over capital, and socialism over capitalism (Ross, 2011). His "Tramp" character's humor proved to be immensely popular with the new film audience, as he was the first to use comedy as a means of political commentary. Chaplin's sympathy for the working class defined his work and was well received by audiences during the first half of the twentieth century. His films were filled with both humor and biting social commentary. In 1932, Chaplin, who to this point had avoided overt political activity, used his stardom to back FDR and his New Deal program, breaking his floodgate to back other leftist candidates, such as Socialist-turned-Democrat California gubernatorial candidate, Upton Sinclair. However, while his 1940 film *The Great Dictator* served as a visual alert of Hitler's persecution of the Jews, Chaplin discovered that audiences did not want film figures to burst their illusions of this movie fantasy world. Audiences flocked to films that distracted them from troubling stories in the news. During this war time, audiences wanted films that supported a patriotic agenda, and criticizing the government earned you the hatred of Americans, especially when films were coupled with the actor's off-screen comments such as "patriotism is the greatest insanity the world has ever suffered" (Ross, 2001, p. 32). What Chaplin saw as "actions in defense of democracy" others saw quite differently (Ross, 2011). Chaplin's pro-communism views drew public criticism for decades, worsening as polarization grew, tying to the alleged Communist infiltration of Hollywood during the 1930s and 1940s. Audiences didn't want their film fantasies to be darkened by controversial politics, and the government didn't want film stars promoting pro-Communist political agendas as the nation was immersed in the Red Scare and subsequent anti-Red hysteria. Backlash worsened for Hollywood leftists in the late 1940s as they became fully entrenched in the House Un-American Activities Committee (HUAC). The U.S. Congress began investigating Communist infiltration and identifying political collaborators in Hollywood. In 1951, hundreds of suspected Hollywood writers, actors, producers, and directors were placed on a "blacklist," banned from industry employment, as the government feared the power of celebrities and their propaganda to influence the way audiences thought and acted (figure 4.1).

HOLLYWOOD'S REPUBLICAN PARTY AND THE BIRTH OF THE CONSERVATIVE MOVEMENT

While the long-standing notion is that Hollywood has been predominantly leftist, it has, in fact, a longer history of conservatism. Hollywood conservatives were able to take greater liberties than the leftists through their alignment with the Republican Party and its main players, as well as in the promotion

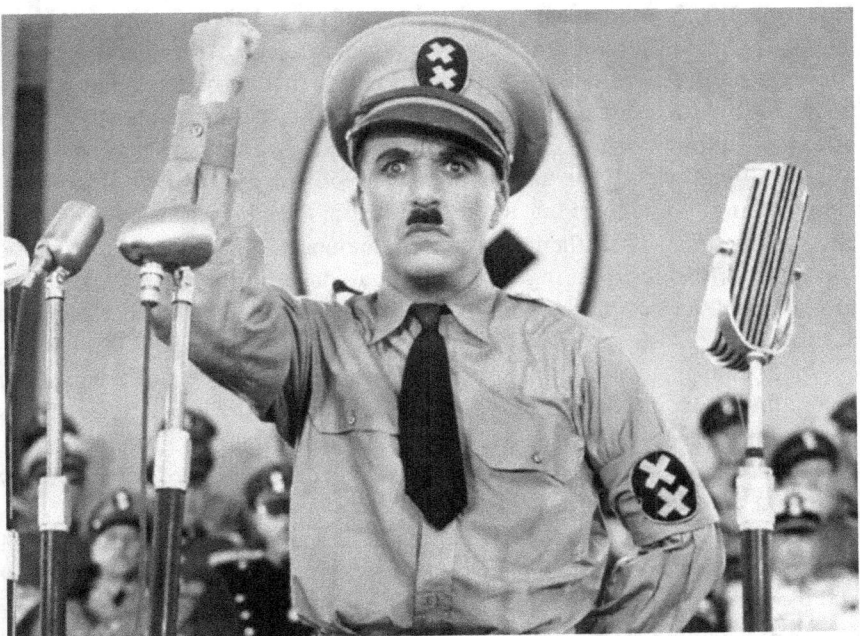

Figure 4.1 Charlie Chaplin, *The Great Dictator*, 1940. *Source*: *The Great Dictator* trailer (1940). *The Great Dictator*. By Trailer screenshot, Public Domain, Retrieved January 16, 2020 https://commons.wikimedia.org/w/index.php?curid=8971705

of films depicting the idea of "true Americanism" (Ross, 2011). No one represented the conservative side of Hollywood more than Louis B. Mayer, of Metro-Goldwyn-Mayer (MGM), "the man who brought the Republican Party to Hollywood and Hollywood to the Republican Party" (Ross, 2011, p. 52). In this depression era, his films reflected his visions of hope, optimism, and everything he saw as right in American. His films created an old-fashioned world, depicting his values of "Family, God and Country" and rejecting the collectivist ideals of the New Deal. He offered people the view of America that he felt they wanted to see, which was not necessarily the "real" America (Ross, 2011).

Most importantly, Mayer brought Hollywood into electoral politics. He created a connection between the business-oriented GOP and the corporate-minded movie industry. Once Mayer was appointed treasurer of the Republican National Committee of California in 1928, Hollywood became a new epicenter for Republican political fundraising, which was becoming more and more important as the influx of radio brought with it higher advertising costs. Mayer's greatest contribution to politics (and specifically, the Republican Party) was to insert showmanship and celebrity (Ross, 2011). He worked with politicians, applying his Hollywood skillset. Mayer helped get both Calvin Coolidge and Herbert Hoover elected president. Prior to Mayer's involvement in politics, political leaders hadn't realized that politics could be a show. Mayer, however, recognized that an audience is an audience, and like moviegoers, voters wanted a good show, and he knew how to make it that way. He is the originator of much of what we see in political campaigning today, teaching Republican candidates how to use radio, film, and movie stars to sell their message to audiences. Mayer also understood the appeal of celebrity, bringing with him a consortium of Hollywood stars to every political event, the origins of the star-studded political events we see today.

Under Mayer's leadership, some of these stars even began having their own political aspirations, as Mayer began to work on the Republican Party's long-term prospects. He used MGM studio into a "training ground" for the Republican Party, educating and courting actors on a variety of contemporary issues, in an effort to turn them into Republican activists (Ross, 2011). His efforts not only solicited celebrity participation, but also in the beginnings of celebrities interested in leadership that would guide both the movie industry and the country. His efforts initiated a succession of powerful celebrity leaders. Like Chaplin, Mayer's run in Hollywood came to an end as the societal climate changed and his political views no longer aligned with his studio, but he left behind a legacy of Hollywood conservatism, culminating in the mid-1960s elections of actor-turned senator George Murphy and actor-turned governor Ronald Reagan.

MOVEMENT POLITICS OF THE 1960S AND 1970S

During the 1960s and 1970s, celebrities were key figures in ushering in an era of movement politics, grassroots mass movement to promote a common ideology to initiate drastic revolution. Unlike short-term endorsement, movement politics was a long-term commitment, working for decades to bring radical change and turn their grassroots efforts and ideas into national policy. At this time, movement politics was growing on both the left and right, and celebrities were at the forefront on both sides.

On the right, George Murphy and Ronald Reagan brought a new type of leadership. As elected officials, they aimed to alter the foundation of American government, beginning with overturning the New Deal (Ross, 2011). For them, they saw the best way to do this as holding political office. On the left, it was celebrities like Harry Belafonte, Jane Fonda, Paul Newman, and Warren Beatty who used their celebrity to lead marches, mass demonstrations, picket lines, and sit-ins to protest the Vietnam War and advocate for civil rights change. Similarly, Charlton Heston fell on both sides of the political spectrum at times, active in the left-leaning civil rights movement, and taking the lead in celebrity activism on the right.

Both Murphy and Reagan were products of Mayer's brand of politics, combining their decades of involvement with Republican groups with their years of experience as actors. Reagan and Murphy followed in Mayer's footsteps and used visual production, for them, TV rather than the movies of Mayer's time. They were able to make conservatism acceptable to voters, using their celebrity (the charisma that made them celebrities to begin with) to sell it to skeptical voters. Their elections indicated the beginning of America's attitude toward celebrities and politics, namely that they had a right to be political (Ross, 2011). Both of these actor-turned politicians began as liberal Democrats and switched to conservative Republicans, taking America with them and leading this long-term movement for decades. Mayer's influence culminated in Reagan's time in the White House, twenty years later (figure 4.2).

Civil Rights and Vietnam

The celebrity influence in movement politics, perfected by Murphy and Reagan, became the central focus of celebrity involvement on the left, as vocal celebrities served as figureheads for civil rights and Vietnam activism.

During the late 1950s, actor-singer Harry Belafonte was Hollywood's hottest black celebrity. When asked by Reverend Dr. Martin Luther King, Jr. to help him in his civil rights mission, Belafonte put his career on hold to help King fight to transform race relations. Unlike Murphy and Reagan,

Figure 4.2 Ronald Reagan and General Electric Theater, 1954–62. *Source*: General Electric (n.d.) Ronald Reagan at General Electric Theater. Retrieved January 18, 2020, from https://commons.wikimedia.org/wiki/File:Ronald_Reagan_and_General_Electric _Theater_1954-62.jpg

who were at the same time highly visible in the conservative movement, Belafonte chose to "remain under the radar" in an effort to keep the spotlight on civil rights rather than on his celebrity (Ross, 2011). Even with his subvert activism with King, Belafonte still thought of himself as an actor first, and he was dedicated to making movies that moved beyond racial stereotypes and changed the way society looked at race. He wanted to use film to open audiences' minds and change the overall national consciousness about race. Belafonte continued to work with King, and worked to plan the March on Washington (figure 4.3).

The Hollywood March committee was led by Charlton Heston, who later fought battles, unpopular to the left, opposing affirmative action, big

Figure 4.3 Sammy Davis Jr. at Civil Rights March in Washington, 1963. *Source*: U.S. Information Agency. Press and Publications Service (ca. 1953–ca. 1978). This media is available in the holdings of the National Archives and Records Administration, cataloged under the National Archives Identifier (NAID) 542050., Public Domain, https://commons.wikimedia.org/w/index.php?curid=149908

government, and gun control (Ross, 2011). Heston led sixty big-name Hollywood stars, including Sammy Davis Jr., Paul Newman, and Marlon Brando, as they joined King in Washington for the March on Washington in 1963. His transformation to activist on the right happened later, becoming the biggest conservative Hollywood celebrity of the 1980s and 1990s.

After civil rights, movement politics on the left focused on the Vietnam War, with celebrities such as Jane Fonda leading the effort. Fonda took over for Belafonte, becoming "Hollywood's most dominant movement leader" (Ross, 2011, p. 227). Unlike Belafonte's "under the radar" approach to activism, Fonda made it her goal to become highly visible, working as both an activist and an organizer, using her celebrity to garner attention. Fonda, the earliest female actor/activist, earned criticism that her male counterparts avoided. We see her efforts in today's era of celebrity activism, such as in #metoo (as we'll discuss in chapter 6), yet she was attacked by media and given labels such as "Cause Celeb" and "Queen Mother of celebrity politics," and "Hanoi Jane," while conservatives displayed bumper stickers saying, "I'm NOT FONDA JANE" (Ross, 2011, p. 228). Male celebrities didn't see these responses to their activism, yet by 1980, *World Almanac* ranked her as the nation's fifth most influential woman, not celebrity, but woman (figure 4.4).

Though not as involved in the grassroots movement politics of Vietnam, and definitely not as hated as Fonda, actor Warren Beatty also used the issue to further his involvement in politics. In line with the movement, Beatty did fight to bring major change. His beginnings in politics go back to the *Brown v. Board of Education* decision in 1954, when he became interested in the beginning of desegregation (Ross, 2011). His movie career echoed his off-screen political interests, starting the *Bonnie and Clyde*, about which he expressed an antiauthoritarian view that sympathized with the difficulty of ordinary people, similar to Charlie Chaplin (Ross, 2011).

Beatty's biggest political contributions, however, were off camera, behind the scenes, Harry Belafonte style, campaigning for Robert Kennedy. George McGovern was also pleased to befriend Beatty and have his support, as he

Figure 4.4 Jane Fonda, 1975. *Source*: Dutch National Archives, The Hague, Fotocollectie Algemeen Nederlands Persbureau (ANeFo), 1945-1989, Nummer toegang 2.24.01.07 Bestanddeelnummer 254-9554

recognized the value movie stars brought to a campaign. He spoke of the "ripple effect" celebrity attention brought, and that celebrity involvement "raised my morale and the morale of our workers, volunteers and staff people"; and that it gave them all "a lift to have these celebrities involved" (Ross, 2011, p. 326). This effect was exemplified in the political rock concert on the eve of the California primary, when Beatty organized a celebrity-filled event that raised nearly $300,000 and won McGovern the Democratic nomination.

Talk of Beatty running for political office circled for decades. He worked closely on Gary Hart's campaigns for president in 1984 and 1988, which led to speculation about his political career. He continued bringing his politics to the silver screen with movies such as *Reds* (1981) and *Bulworth* (1998), a critique of American politics, which he hoped would cause a paradigm shift back to an activist state of politics—an attack on party politics. He used promotion of the film to critique campaign finance reform, class inequity, and the failures of the Democratic Party. He was critical that the Democratic Party had become too much like the Republican Party. He even began calling himself a "Bulworth Democrat," and there began talk of "putting Bulworth in the White House" (Ross, 2011). He continued on his exploration path to potentially run for president in 2001, but opted not to seek office, ultimately not wanting to give up Hollywood and his privacy for Washington.

"GOVERNATOR": ARNOLD SCHWARZENEGGER AND THE GROWTH OF ENTERTAINMENT NEWS

In 2003, bodybuilder-turned-actor Arnold Schwarzenegger took celebrity politics to a new level when he followed in Ronald Reagan's footsteps and made the move from Hollywood to the California governor's office. Unlike Reagan, however, Arnold was a political newcomer, with barely any political background. Arnold became heavily involved in the campaign of George H. W. Bush, who referred to him as "Conan the Republican," after one of Arnold's prominent characters, Conan the Barbarian. His role in the Bush campaign led to his subsequent appointment by Bush as the chairman of the President's Council on Physical Fitness, in which he spent the next few years targeting the wellness and fitness of American families and, especially, its children.

In addition to his bodybuilder/movie star fame, his greatest political ties came through his marriage to TV journalist (and fellow celebrity) Maria Shriver, daughter of Sargeant and Eunice Kennedy Shriver of the Kennedy Family. He married Shriver during his time in the Bush administration. The Shrivers gave Arnold advice to follow if he hoped to advance his political career: alter his action hero persona to line up with the political values he espoused (Ross, 2011). Embracing Bush's political agenda, Arnold shifted his movies to those that evoked less action hero and more compassionate conservative, thinking about his long-term political aspirations. Family-friendly movies such as *Kindergarten Cop* (1988) and *Twins* (1990) were hardly political in their content, but they were a good opportunity to increase his visibility with a different sect and aligned with his long-term goals. He also used his Hollywood style to excite crowds at his political rallies. He used references to and lines from his movies, playing up lines like "Hasta la vista, baby" (figure 4.5).

Without much of a political background, Arnold didn't have an established platform or political network, but he had name recognition, which he used to draw attention to his campaign for California governor in 2003. Arnold knew that he wasn't a traditional candidate, and, therefore, he couldn't run a traditional political campaign, so he opted to use entertainment news, rather than traditional media outlets, to reach his fans and the public. He used his stardom and celebrity skills to make politics entertaining to audiences who wouldn't ordinarily be interested. He announced his candidacy for California governor on *The Tonight Show with Jay Leno*, campaigned on *Oprah*, and realized the importance of the influx of the 24/7 entertainment news world of *E!, Access Hollywood, Entertainment Tonight* and celebrity news websites. He continued what Bill Clinton's 1991 appearance playing the saxophone on *The Arsenio Hall Show* began—innovatively using entertainment media as campaigning tools. He realized that while entertainment news would not replace traditional media, it was important in its own right. It was a new way to engage voters and bolster the image side of their candidacy. Entertainment news programs allowed candidates, like Arnold, to show a different side of themselves to those viewers who used it as a supplement to traditional media, as well as reach voters who watched entertainment news but eschewed traditional news.

Arnold inoculated audiences to all that he anticipated being thrown at him on his visit to *The Tonight Show with Jay Leno*, when he told audiences "I know they're going to throw everything at me and they're going, you know, to say that I have no experience and that I'm a womanizer and that I'm a terrible guy . . . (but) I want to clean up Sacramento. I want to go in there and reform the system so it's back in the people's hands. . . . I'm going to pump California up" (Ross, 2011, p. 394). Leno drew its highest ratings in years, and the audience loved it, and Arnold. He continued this message throughout his campaign: he was not a typical candidate or a traditional politician, and he wasn't going to campaign through traditional media, eventually using this message and his celebrity to sell himself to voters and win the California gubernatorial race. He took the oath of office with 130 television cameras covering it, including *E!, Entertainment Tonight, Access Hollywood*, and other entertainment shows that had never covered an inauguration, making the event seem more like a Hollywood movie premiere. Although his next seven years in office were deemed by many as a failure, his campaign success

Figure 4.5 **"The Governator Ahh-nold."** *Source*: Flickr (n.d.). Governator Ahh-nold. Retrieved January 16, 2020, from https://images.app.goo.gl/zNzRQcPC4b7rvCyB8

showed the importance of entertainment politics and engaging the potential voters who typically don't vote and aren't interested in politics through the media that they enjoy.

CELEBRITIES AND TWENTY-FIRST-CENTURY ACTIVISM

In the twenty-first century, celebrities have become even more visible in the political spotlight, and the Hollywood-Washington connection has further developed many facets. Celebrities become politicians, politicians become celebrities, celebrities champion causes and endorse politicians, and both causes and politicians need celebrity activism to succeed. They have both joined existing activist campaigns and actively initiated causes of their own (Marks & Fischer, 2002). A number of celebrities have hired political consultants to advise them on various policy and lobbying issues (Smillie, 1998). Formal and informal networks exist to make the connection between celebrities and political causes—like a "political dating agency" (Street, 2002).

Not only are celebrities eager to get involved with political causes and candidates, but causes are anxious to have celebrity representation. Activism can bring a star both personal satisfaction and respectability, and the causes and candidates get money and media attention, the two things they need most (Smillie, 1998). A celebrity face makes that particular candidate or cause stand out in a sea of political causes. Celebrities are assumed to symbolize authority "for no other reason than their seeming ability to rise above the noise of participatory democracy" (Marks & Fischer, 2002, p. 385). Smillie (1998) suggested that celebrities and politicians offer each other something that they individually lack; elected officials have credibility, but are often not liked; and celebrities are well liked and admired, but don't often have credibility or respectability to their names. Even if celebrity endorsements don't translate directly into votes, the money they raise should translate into support (Moore, 2007).

Street (2002) explained that social movements need celebrities to legitimize their causes, and celebrities do this by lending both their celebrity and popularity to them. Causes need someone to represent them to the world, and who better to do that than a famous face? Politics is a world of social networks, and celebrities have some of the largest and most influential networks. Once a cause attracts the attention of a celebrity, that celebrity will recruit others through his or her own social network (Street, 2002). For example, as we discussed in chapter 3, celebrity-filled get-out-the-vote campaigns of the early 2000s drew an assortment of performers to them, often becoming partisan events. During the 2004 campaign, Bruce Springsteen supported John Kerry for president. Through Springsteen's ties, the star-studded Vote for Change concert tour began, including Dave Matthews, R.E.M., the Dixie Chicks, Pearl Jam, and Bonnie Raitt. In 2008, Springsteen again stumped for the Democratic candidate, this time headlining fundraising concerts for Obama, with tickets costing upward of $10,000, as well as his inauguration concert on the National Mall. The influential role of social media, namely Twitter, in 2012 added a new dimension to the role of celebrities in campaigns. Twitter not only made it easier for politicians, celebrities, and journalists to reach out to huge amount of voters, but it also made it easier for voters, candidates, and analysts to calculate the influence of a celebrity endorsement by judging the number of followers of that celebrity (Wong, 2012). Regardless of how any of it translates to votes or actual support and participation, between followers and retweets, Twitter lends itself especially well to monitoring and assessing the perception of others' views and the potential for influencing public opinion (figure 4.6).

Marks and Fischer (2002) suggested that people are increasingly taking their cues from celebrity activists. The political climate has shifted to one that is conducive to celebrity activism. First, traditional social movement leaders' power to incite has diminished. Celebrities now lead the media spectacles meant to draw attention to a cause. Second, activists no longer represent grassroots movements; instead, important issues and celebrity endorsements are now synonymous and social movements must share the spotlight with Hollywood celebrities (Marks & Fischer, 2002).

Unfortunately, although celebrity involvement in politics often leaves the public entertained, it has been argued that this "celebrification" or "trivialization" of politics does little for the serious discussion of policy (Feldmann, 1999, p. 1). During the past decades, American culture has grown increasingly celebrity focused. Life, itself, has become entertainment oriented. Most American institutions are now driven by entertainment (Gabler, 1998). Politics is no different. Marks and Fischer (2002) argued that the shift to a celebrity-driven activism depicts a fundamental shift of power in the United States, which reflects a simulated system of government; the media serve as a

Figure 4.6 2004 Vote for Change Concert in Washington DC, Featuring Dave Matthews, John Fogerty, Eddie Vedder, and Bruce Springsteen. *Source*: Cannon, A. (2003). The showbiz connection. U.S. News & World Report, 135, 22-23. By Davis, Davis, J. (n.d.). Photography from United States of America—Vote for Change, CC BY-SA 2.0, https://commons.wikimedia.org/w/index.php?curid=68756792

means for real democracy to be replaced by a simulated one. The researchers explained that the media deploy celebrities to simulate the public's political consent. The American culture is becoming more accepting of celebrity political agendas. People often rely on celebrities in part to help them become politically knowledgeable (Marks & Fischer, 2002). In chapter 6, we'll discuss the role that celebrities are playing in setting the political agenda and making their fans politically knowledgeable post-2016.

Little scholarly research addresses the public's perception of celebrity activists or the effects that they have on society. Do celebrity endorsements make a difference? Did they make a difference in these presidential elections? Reports are conflicting. Some say no, reporting that less than 10 percent of people were influenced by a celebrity endorsement in the 2004 election (Maurstad, 2004). However, MediaVest (2004) reported that 40 percent of young adults eighteen to twenty-four years old were influenced by celebrity endorsements, and 15 percent of all adults reported a celebrity influence on their voting preferences. If nothing else, celebrity endorsements may impact young people as a "stepping stone activist experience"; they attend a concert because Springsteen is playing, and they stay to take part in the political activity of it (Duncombe, 2007). Our nation's youth often show an apathetic attitude toward voting and find politics wasteful and boring (Payne, Hanson & Tworney, 2007). Celebrities attract attention wherever they go and whatever they do. If not translating directly to votes, they bring a candidate or cause both media attention and fundraising money. Celebrity involvement increases the chances of audiences paying attention and being persuaded. Maybe celebrity-driven campaigns are what is needed to take notice and act. In chapter 5, we'll look at the highly celebrity-driven campaigns of 2016, and in chapter 6, we'll see how 2016 was only the start.

REFERENCES

Baker, R. K. (2007, December 26). Celebrity endorsements are not always good politics. *USA Today*, p. 9A.

Cannon, A. (2003). The showbiz connection. *U. S. News & World Report*, 135, 22–23.

Davis, D. J. (n.d.). *Photography from United States of America—Vote for Change, CC BY-SA 2.0*. https://commons.wikimedia.org/w/index.php?curid=68756792.

Duncombe, S. (2007, October 29). Taking celebrity seriously. *The Nation*, pp. 22–24.

Feldmann, L. (1999). America's new celebrity culture. *Christian Science Monitor*, 91, 1.

Flickr. (n.d.). *Governator Ahh-Nold*. Retrieved January 16, 2020, from https://images.app.goo.gl/zNzRQcPC4b7rvCyB8.

Gabler, N. (1998). *Life the Movie: How Entertainment Conquered Reality*. New York, NY: Knopf.

General Electric. (n.d.). *Ronald Reagan at General Electric Theater*. Retrieved January 18, 2020, from https://commons.wikimedia.org/wiki/File:Ronald_Reagan_and_General_Electric_Theater_1954-62.jpg.

Grier, P., & McLaughlin, A. (2003). Politics as another rung on celebrity ladder. *Christian Science Monitor*, 95, 1. Retrieved March 22, 2005, from Academic Search Premier.

The Great Dictator Trailer. (1940). *The Great Dictator*. By Trailer Screenshot, Public Domain. Retrieved January 16, 2020 https://commons.wikimedia.org/w/index.php?curid=8971705.

Marks, M. P., & Fischer, Z. M. (2002). The king's new bodies: Simulating consent in the age of celebrity. *New Political Science*, 24, 371–395.

Maurstad, T. (2004, February 4). From Hollywood to Washington: Blurring the lines between politics and pop culture. *The Dallas Morning News*, p. A3.

MediaVest USA. (2004, September 30). *Word to Presidential Hopefuls: Celebrities on Campaign Trail Reach Young Voters*. Retrieved March 22, 2005, from http://www.mediaweek.com.

Mieremet, Rob/Anefo. (1975). *Dutch National Archives, The Hague, Fotocollectie Algemeen Nederlands Persbureau (ANeFo), 1945–1989, Nummer toegang 2.24.01.07 Bestanddeelnummer 254-9554, CC BY-SA 3.0 nl*. https://commons.wikimedia.org/w/index.php?curid=32335014.

Moore, M. T. (2007, October 22). Oprah becomes test of what an endorsement means. *USA Today*, p. 1A.

Payne, J. G., Hanlon, J. P., & Tworney, D. P. (2007). Celebrity spectacle influence on young voters in the 2004 presidential campaign. *American Behavioral Scientist*, 50, 1239–1246.

Richter, G. (2013). *Jane Fonda: I Will Go to My Grave with "Unforgivable Mistake."* Retrieved April 29, 2019, from https://www.newsmax.com/Newsfront/Jane-Fonda-unforgivable-mistake/2013/04/03/id/497721/.

Ross, S. J. (2011). *Hollywood Left and Right: How Movie Stars Shaped American Politics*. New York, NY: Oxford University Press.

Schwab, N. (2014). *Author: Acting Set Stage for Ronald Reagan's Biggest Role*. Retrieved April 26, 2019, from https://www.usnews.com/news/blogs/washington-whispers/2014/09/25/author-acting-set-stage-for-ronald-reagans-biggest-role.

Smillie, D. (2004). Activism is entertainers' new role. *Christian Science Monitor*, 90, B1. Retrieved March 22, 2005, from Academic Search Premier.

Street, J. (2002). Bob, Bono, and Tony B: The popular artist as politician. *Media, Culture, & Society*, 23, 433–441.

U.S. Information Agency. Press and Publications Service (ca. 1953–ca. 1978). *This Media is Available in the Holdings of the National Archives and Records Administration, Cataloged under the National Archives Identifier (NAID) 542050*, Public Domain. https://commons.wikimedia.org/w/index.php?curid=149908.

Wong, V. (2012). *Obama vs Romney Celebrity Endorsements: Why Stars Continue to Shine in Election 2012*. Retrieved March 22, 2014, from http://www.policymic.com/articles.

Chapter 5

Election 2016

The Celebrity Election

The 2016 presidential election defied conventional political marketing practices, as two very different yet strikingly similar candidates—neither appearing presidential, touting politically correct positions, possessing political experience, or even appearing qualified to run for office—took the country by storm with their populist messages, emotional themes, and strong branding practices. Alongside them was a third candidate, who followed a much more traditional path, marketing and otherwise. While Donald Trump and Bernie Sanders are philosophically and politically different, from a marketing and branding perspective, they were very close in spirit. Both candidates used populist narratives, created strong brands, motivated supporters with a "revolution," and utilized social media, while blaming the media and party for the "perceived unfairness and rigging of the entire system" (Gillies, 2018, p. 97), whereas Hillary Clinton used more traditional marketing practices, delivering high-density policy speeches and anti-Trump messages to appeal to educated, moderate swing voters (Elder, 2018).

In this chapter, we'll look at political marketing in the 2016 presidential election. To fully understand the landscape, we'll include three candidates, Donald Trump, Hillary Clinton, and Bernie Sanders, specifically addressing their individual brands, as well as how Trump rebranded the Republican Party. Rather than traditional political marketing strategy, the market-driven politics of this campaign is highly representative of IMC, as we discussed in chapter 1. Whereas Hillary Clinton maintained a more traditional marketing four Ps approach, Donald Trump took an IMC approach, focusing on the four Cs. Finally, we'll discuss the 2016 as the celebrity election, with Trump serving as more of a celebrity than a politician, and Clinton returning us back to the roots, as discussed in chapter 4, where politicians were our celebrities. If that wasn't enough celebrification, the 2016 election was flooded with celebrity endorsements—most on the Clinton side—which Clinton embraced and Trump eschewed, despite his prior celebrity relationships during his pre-political years.

POLITICAL MARKETING IN THE 2016 ELECTION

The 2016 presidential campaign changed political marketing. Today's voters are more demanding and divided than ever, and successful political campaigners must modify their strategies to keep up with this changed electorate. Donald Trump's presidential campaign successfully accomplished this by challenging conventional political marketing paradigms, theories, and frameworks. He took advantage of the shifting party-voter relationship, and managed to defy traditional calls for personal legitimacy and political credibility. The Trump campaign recognized the value of connective emotional themes, which appealed to a particular group of voters, providing him a path to victory. He acknowledged that new era voters don't need to be encouraged to vote; they're highly motivated. Rather, campaigns must be aware of and responsive to their demands, as they vote based more on emotion than reason.

Today's political media environment makes it difficult for candidates to create a one-size-fits-all coherent political agenda, as the media environment becomes more fragmented and segmented, allowing voters to find their specialized niches. Beginning during the Republican primary, Trump successfully managed this by developing messaging tactics designed for smaller, more targeted audiences. His core message was based on a detailed, research-driven understanding of the consumer voter segments he was trying to reach (Conley, 2018). While this is standard campaign practice, Trump categorically demonstrated the strength of a targeted consumer-based strategy. His technique was unique in that he attempted to formulate policy and communicate that policy based on representing what targeted groups of voters believed and wanted without any effort to interact with or shape those opinions; he only mimicked them (Conley, 2018). Trump first determined his target audiences, and through market research, he assessed what they wanted to hear, and then crafted his messages accordingly.

Clinton, on the other hand, took a more traditional candidate-driven campaigning approach, working in the reverse order from Trump. She first determined why she got into politics, what she hoped to accomplish, what issues she believed were the most important, and what she and her campaign stood for, and then she thought strategically about the voter segments to target and how to reach them, crafting messages accordingly (Conley, 2018). Clinton believed that these segments were the vast majority of Democratic voters, but during the primaries, Sanders recognized the more forgotten segments of the

Democratic Party. He took over the Democrats by capitalizing on targeting the portion that Clinton believed was a fringe of the party, but, in actuality, was a sizable portion. He tapped into disaffected progressives, income inequality warriors, millennial and younger voters, and white working-class voters who had become disillusioned with the Democratic Party (Gillies, 2018). Once in the general election, Clinton was unable to make her established message successfully reach these group, with some turning to Trump, and others just not voting.

Clinton's messaging itself was starkly different than Trump's, again taking a more traditional approach. She was a typical presidential candidate through and through, playing the political game, whereas both Trump and Sanders—although Sanders was clearly less successful—defied the odds by refusing to play by the rules of that game. Everything about Clinton's campaign followed standard political practices. She wrote carefully scripted, complex messages, targeting an educated voter. Every word was carefully planned out, and it was clear which voters she was trying to target. Trump, instead of using carefully planned messages, built his following through what appeared to be improvised speech, often via his personal social media platforms. Although Trump's messages appeared to be on-the-fly and instantaneous, they were actually part of a carefully constructed research-driven marketing strategy that was years in the making (Conley, 2018). This strategy of "speaking the truth" and "saying what he thinks" was Trump's most effective marketing tool, as Clinton was criticized for appearing too calculated in her campaigning.

Trump wrote to a sixth-grade level, and his use of low-level language was a key part of making both himself and his brand relatable to his target consumers (Cosgrove, 2018). He spoke directly to voters, both figuratively in the language he chose and literally through his reliance on social media, which drew a direct contrast to Clinton and other political elites. Again, Trump knew the audience he wanted to reach and mimicked the way they would want him to reach them. While his language and messages were repellant to those who it was not aimed, it fit perfectly with his target consumer base's emotions and values (Cosgrove, 2018). Trump created a narrative that he was outside of the system, a wealthy businessman who couldn't be bought by special interests, while he simultaneously crafted the narrative that Clinton herself was the system. This tactic instilled loyalty and enthusiasm among these supporters and crafted a brand that Clinton couldn't escape.

Trump perpetuated this narrative and created a brand that took on a life of its own and became a living thing, generating enthusiasm among supporters through a barrage of staged events, unprecedented usage of social media and a reliance on earned and nontraditional media. Earned media was the media coverage that the Trump campaign generated without paying for it.

Nontraditional media refers to his reaching out to voters through entertainment television and sports radio programming, similar to strategies employed by the Bill Clinton and Obama campaigns. Trump's incessant use of social media, like Twitter, especially in its often attacking and negative tone, and these nontraditional media appearances, generated him enough earned media to reach voters, while decreasing the need to purchase traditional media advertising. Again, this was a consumer-driven strategy, as Trump's campaign recognized that voters, especially the groups that he was targeting, didn't trust traditional media outlets and instead, they trusted the off-the-cuff quality of social media and nontraditional sources as a channel for receiving political information (figure 5.1).

Both Trump and Sanders were able to use a heavy social media presence to generate enthusiasm and comradery among their supporters. The candidates consistently branded their campaigns with the hashtags #MAGA and #FeelTheBern, an integral part of social media strategy. These strong hashtags generated more exposure for posts from and about the campaign and its events and were an effective way to engage audiences. The hashtags and their related slogans, Make America Great Again and Feel the Bern, plus an assortment of merch (i.e., campaign merchandise), such as the red MAGA hat, created a strong sense of community, online and face-to-face,

Figure 5.1 Donald Trump, 2016, "Make America Great Again". *Source*: Skidmore, G. (2016). Donald Trump Make America Great Again image. Retrieved January 17, 2020, from https://www.flickr.com/photos/gageskidmore/25927662706

among members of their targeted consumer groups. As they began to use the hashtags and buy and wear the merch (which also was an excellent source of fundraising for the campaigns), consumers felt drawn into the campaign, feeling ego involved and identifying with their respective brands.

BRANDING

Strategically, Trump and Clinton could not have been further apart. Trump and Sanders, however, followed much more similar campaigning paths. As a political native, Clinton used her political lineage and background to project a brand of control and competence. After paying her dues for many years in a variety of political roles, she was always the presumptive front runner and Democratic nominees. Her brand became that of an experienced political elite, although, that was a brand created more by Trump than by Clinton herself. Trump created the narrative that Clinton was tied to elite business and political interests. She didn't have effective responses to these attacks, which allowed him to define her on these issues. He painted her as the enemy to a large group of white, working-class voters, many of whom were registered Democrats (Conley, 2018). Simultaneously, he created a populist-nationalist brand for himself.

Both Trump and Sanders branded themselves as outsiders who were beyond the system and who refused to follow the established decorum of campaigning. Meanwhile, Trump himself was creating a brand that included being the stereotypical politically incorrect white male who was fed up with a controlling government and controlling women; the narrative he created personified Clinton as both (Conley, 2018). Trump's brand included his willingness to offend, his swagger and his self-assurance, which allowed Trump to gain attention through earned media to establish a strong base of support among large groups of disenchanted Americans who felt that they have been left behind by the political and economic system. His willingness to defame his opponents and launch personal attacks against anyone who stood in his way, defied everything a presidential candidate's brand is supposed to be; this won the appreciation of his supporters as someone they saw as bucking political convention (Conley, 2018). He appeared to be more trustworthy to voters, while simultaneously making Clinton appear less so. Part of each candidate's brand is their credibility, which is a multidimensional assessment by voters based primarily on experience, trustworthiness, and goodwill. While Clinton had the experience component, Trump's brand of an authentic outsider and Clinton's brand of being a political elite weighted credibility in his favor.

While Clinton's brand started and stopped at her, Trump and Sanders recognized that today's voters want more than a candidate. They want a movement—a revolution—and Clinton felt like a predictable outcome rather than a revolution. Movement politics suggests that successful politics begins with effective ideological movements, and that those movements are essential to any serious political gain. Campaigns based on movements, ideology, and ideas are much more powerful than voters' allegiances to any political party. For Trump, his personality was his biggest attribute, and for Sanders, his messaging became more important than the candidate himself (Gillies, 2018). For both, the party brand was secondary, and they found ways to reach voters directly without the party apparatus, but for Clinton, that was all she had. In today's political climate where consumers are basing their decisions more on their emotions and what they believe is "right," they're grasping on to brands that include something more—brands that include a movement. Whether it is Starbucks taking a stand to protect the environment through the reduction of one-time use plastic or Trump taking a stand to protect our jobs through immigration reform or Sanders taking a stand to protect working families through tax reform, consumers want to be part of something bigger than themselves. Trump and Sanders understood that their branding needed to be centered around a mass movement idea, making voters feel as if they are part of a movement or revolution. Trump's movement was personality and culturally driven, whereas Sanders' movement was idea-driven; Clinton, however, had neither type behind her, and therefore, voters saw her as being an inauthentic insider politician running against the movement-driven antipoliticians (Gillies, 2018).

THE FOUR PS OF CLINTON AND FOUR CS OF TRUMP

In chapter 1, we addressed IMC's migration from a product-based marketing approach to a consumer-oriented IMC approach. Unlike the traditional model where the primary focus is on the product and products are developed and pushed on the consumer, IMC's primary focus is on the consumer. In the 2016 election, Clinton's campaign was traditional and product based, whereas Trump's campaign was consumer oriented. Just as with a commercial product, the Clinton campaign developed her as a candidate in a way for which they anticipated the Democratic candidate should be. Then, they placed a perceived value on this candidate and made consumers aware through what the campaign saw as historically the best communication channels to reach their target audience. She was a candidate created based on an idea, and then put forward to voters to hopefully accept and support.

Trump's campaign took a different approach, studying consumer behavior and applying market research, and then developing him as a candidate based on the consumer's demand. To successfully market Trump to consumers, the candidate had to be conveniently placed. Social and earned media provided that constant avenue into voters' purview. As opposed to Clinton's traditional marketing focus of straight promotion, Trump's IMC approach placed a higher value on his brand, specifically, communication of that brand to create a brand awareness and brand recognition. He knew that utilizing the most effective communication strategies and methods for segmenting, targeting, and positioning him as a product based on the brand and his target audience for that brand was crucial to success. He accomplished this with his Twitter posts and website updates to directly address his audience, his #MAGA hashtag to generate exposure, his merch to brand and create a sense of community, and his large rallies to motivate his supporters. Additionally, Trump used a similar approach to merge the branding of him as a candidate with a rebranding of the Republican Party.

REBRANDING: THE REPUBLICAN PARTY REBRAND AND TRUMP

In chapter 1, we discussed rebranding, and that to remain successful, sometimes, political parties need to rebrand in an effort to respond to the times and change with consumer demand. Rebranding can involve a full rebrand, redefining the entire brand identity, or a partial rebrand, focusing on a refresh or update. In 2016, Trump solved the problem of a "stale Republican brand and declining market share" with a rebrand of the Republican Party (Cosgrove, 2018, p. 50). To do so, he combined the established Trump brand with Reagan's branding, including updating Reagan's 1980's logo in more modern, technology savvy, hues and relaunching his tag line, "Make American Great Again," and then he developed the brand to be more populist, while bringing back the anger that Nixon and Wallace had used in the late 1960s and early 1970s (Cosgrove, 2018). Trump's rebrand for the Republican Party was centered around restoring the party to a greatness that he believed had been lost through the failed party philosophies of "Compassionate Conservatism" and "Country First" of the 1990s and 2000s. Trump used this rebranding as a path to restore America to the glorious country of the past, "where the rules were followed, the borders were secure, the values of the majority were valued most, both in racial and cultural terms, there was no threat of terrorist violence, and the economy worked for all" (Cosgrove, 2018, p. 49). He believed he knew what the people wanted from the Republican Party and nominee and that he could channel their anger to forge a successful path to the White House.

The Republican Party needed a rebrand because of a series of product failures, because the party's offerings were not appealing to traditional voters and because it needed to find a way to emotionally engage with and turn out its voters (Cosgrove, 2018). The decline of the Republican Party had been going on since the era of George W. Bush, who many conservatives felt betrayed them with his runaway spending habits, and unprovoked invasion of Iraq (Hirsh, 2016). Through the Obama years, the Republican Party had become so disjointed that no one knew what the party really stood for anymore, beyond being anti-Obama. With the loudest voice in the anti-Obama "birther" movement, Trump was the perfect candidate to lead a rebrand that began by establishing a base of Obama-haters, a group of angry, undereducated, working- and middle-class whites who were tired of seeing tax cuts for the rich, and targeting them with a narrative of nationalism and patriotic emotions. His platform was simplistic; his language and policy positions were easy to understand, and the base he was targeting liked it that way. Trump positioned himself as the champion for the forgotten little guy (Cosgrove, 2018). Trump and the Republican rebrand took the existing brand and made it more interesting to voters. Most successfully, he was able to use his party positions to define the presidential race, whether the issue was immigration or trade or corporate tax reform. Throughout the 2016 campaign, Trump often said, "If it weren't for me, you wouldn't even be talking about [fill in the blank]." He set the tone for what the Republican brand stood for and what everyone was talking about.

THE CELEBRITY ELECTION

The Role of Celebrity Endorsers

As we discussed in chapter 4, the relationship between Hollywood and Washington isn't new, and celebrities have taken to endorsing political candidates for decades. The divide between Democrat and Republican celebrity endorsements is always significant, but in 2016, it seemed infinite, as Clinton's celebrity endorsements topped Trump's in both numbers and star power. Numerous A-list celebrities were declaring #imwithher, including Beyonce, Jay Z, LeBron James, Bon Jovi, Katy Perry, Oprah, Samuel L. Jackson, Lena Dunham, Miley Cyrus, Amy Schumer, Chelsea Handler, Whoopi Goldberg, Jon Stewart, Cher, Alec Baldwin, Snoop Dog, Meryl Streep, Arnold Schwarzenegger, Goldie Hawn, Jennifer Lopez, Marc Anthony, Kim Kardashian, Rihanna, Lady Gaga, Ariana Grande, Bruce Springsteen, and Reese Witherspoon. Trump had fewer well-known entertainers in his corner and made fun of Clinton for relying on celebrities. Sarah Palin was Trump's most high-profile endorser, but she wasn't completely alone. Although he did not have a single official endorsement from the year's

100 highest-paid celebrities (O'Malley Greenberg, 2016), Trump did have his own gallery of oddball C-list celebrities and members of the political fringe, such as Roseanne Barr, Ted Nugent, *Duck Dynasty* star Willie Roberston, Jon Voight, Scott Baio, Dennis Rodman, and *The Real Housewives of New Jersey's* Teresa Giudice.

Strategy: Celeb—Clinton

While Hollywood does typically lean left, gaining celebrity endorsements was a strategic maneuver for the Clinton campaign because of her targeted demographic. Celebrities are more than stars of TV, music, and movies. They are influencers on social media, already reaching out to large numbers of young people every day. The eighteen to twenty-four demographic is both one susceptible to celebrity influence and the least likely to vote. Celebrities helped to fill the enthusiasm gap between Trump and Clinton, which was in favor of Trump throughout the entire campaign. If celebrities could inspire this group to get out and vote—and especially, to get out and vote for Clinton—it could have been a strategic advantage for her campaign. In the final weeks of the campaign, Clinton's celebrity backers grew, but in a way that seemed like desperate fear rather than enthusiasm. More than trying to persuade voters to vote for their candidate, celebrities were trying to energize people to go out and vote in certain areas where they felt Clinton needed voters to turn out (figure 5.2).

A key state in the Electoral College count, Ohio, was one of the swing states where Clinton consistently trailed behind Trump in the polls. A-plus-list celebrities were aiming for a high turnout of young voters, similar to the one that Obama benefited from in 2008 and 2012. Strategically, reaching this demographic could have made the difference for Clinton. Beyonce and Jay Z held a Get Out the Vote rally in the crucial state just four days before the election. LeBron James also exerted his star power and influence, introducing her as "President Hillary Clinton" at a rally in Cleveland two days before the election. LeBron's endorsement was an attempt to motivate and gain support for Clinton among young black voters, a demographic that the Clintons struggled with since the 1990s. In the equally crucial swing state of Florida, Jennifer Lopez and Marc Anthony held a concert for Clinton in Miami, where JLo reminded voters that Florida and Miami are home to millions of Latinos, who could make a difference with their vote.

In addition to the live concerts and rallies intended to entertain and excite voters, celebrities used social media to reach their supporters. Beyonce posted an Instagram video in support of Clinton, which has received nearly four million views. It highlighted her hope for her daughter to grow up seeing a woman leading this country, as she declared, "We have to think of the opportunities

JAY Z

AND

SPECIAL GUESTS

11/4/16

CLEVELAND, OHIO

TEXT JAYZ TO 47246 FOR ACCESS TO COMPLIMENTARY TICKETS

Figure 5.2 Jay Z and Friends Concert in Cleveland, 2016. *Source*: Hillary for America (2016). Jay Z and Special Guests. Retrieved January 18, 2020, from https://www.facebook.com/hillaryclinton/photos/a.889773484412515.1073741828.889307941125736/1299113203478539/?type=3&theater, Public Domain, https://commons.wikimedia.org/w/index.php?curid=62418696

for our daughters . . . and that is why, I'm with her." Actress Rachel Bloom led a "We Are the World" style get out the vote ballad filled with celebrity cameos called "HOLY SHIT (You've Got to Vote)." In addition to showing support, the video, in both title and tone, revealed the fear and desperation that Clinton's supporters were feeling in those final weeks of the campaign. Actress Lena Dunham's Funny or Die "Sensual Pantsuit Anthem," showed her unwavering support of Clinton and mocked empty celebrity activism, questioning whether she's "hurting the candidate more than helping." The "Save the Day" voter PSA, featuring Robert Downey Jr., Scarlet Johansson, Don Cheadle, and many more, appeared to be a GOTV PSA, but specifically refers to a "racist, abusive coward who could permanently damage the fabric of our society," which would imply support for Clinton over Trump.

Traditionally, the biggest influence celebrities bring a political campaign is financial, either through campaign contributions or fundraising events. The Federal Election Commission limits individual donations to candidates at $2,700, and many celebrities donated that amount, primarily to the Clinton campaign. A few further donated to Political Action Committees, which don't have a limit. For example, director Steven Spielberg and Dreamworks CEO Jeffrey Katzenberg each donated an additional one million dollars, and director Aaron Sorkin donated a half of a million dollars, to PACs, in addition to their maximum Clinton donation (Oswald, 2016). Additionally, the biggest way that high-profile celebrities can significantly help a campaign is with its fundraising efforts. Donating money to a campaign as part of a raffle to win dinner with a celebrity or a chance to go on stage at a concert makes people more likely to donate than just asking them to donate.

Strategy: Anti-Celeb—Trump

During the campaign, not only was he not endorsed by celebrities, but Trump also spent a significant amount of time fighting them. While it's difficult to keep track of every Twitter celebrity feud, really, it's been "another day, another Twitter feud," we'll walk through a few of his most notable, beginning with, since 2008, the most notable celebrity endorser, Oprah (Giannotta, 2018). After spending a number of his pre-political years friends with Oprah, including his 1998 appearance on her show when he announced that he'd like to run for president some day and his 1999 statement that he wanted Oprah to be his running mate when he did, Trump turned on her after speculation began that she would run against him in 2020, and polls showed that she could beat him (Taylor, 2018). He began by declaring—in a meeting in the Cabinet Room with Congress—that he would definitely beat her if she ran (Klein, 2018), and then, despite her denial that she intended to run, Trump began attacking her as being "very insecure," criticizing her interview style, and daring her to run so he could "expose and defeat" her (Horton, 2018). Oprah acknowledged the attack in an interview, but didn't engage him in a Twitter war.

Rosie O'Donnell, however, has been one to respond, engage, and attack Trump many times, making their decade-long feud even more adversarial. Long before Trump took to Twitter, in 2007, after a decision with the Miss USA pageant, O'Donnell criticized him, firing the first shots. Without Twitter as a platform, Trump went to *People* magazine to respond, calling O'Donnell a "a real loser" and "a woman out of control"; Rosie's "a loser. A real loser. I look forward to taking lots of money from my nice fat little Rosie" (Zaru,

2017). Switching to Twitter around 2011, the Trump/O'Donnell feud only escalated, with them attacking each other personally, physically, and professionally at fairly equal rates. Over the years he has called her "rude, crude, obnoxious and dumb," "mentally sick," "totally irrelevant," "not funny or talented" (Giannotta, 2018). The feud made its 2016 campaign debut in the first Republican presidential primary debate, when Megyn Kelly—yet another Trump's celebrity rival—asked him about his use of language like "fat pigs," "dogs," "slobs," and "disgusting animals" to describe some women, and Trump responded, "only Rosie O'Donnell" (Zaru, 2017). The hostility has only increased since Election Day, only reaching a point of agreement when Trump retweeted O'Donnell's tweet after his firing of FBI director James Comey, saying, "We finally agree on something Rosie."

Although we could also add Joy Behar, Molly Sims, Whoopi Goldberg from *The View*, Megyn Kelly, John Oliver, Anderson Cooper, Jimmy Fallon, and Katie Couric to the list of Trump's feuds with celebrities, his adversaries aren't just with those with talk shows and journalists. Trump has also had notable public celebrity feuds with actors Robert De Niro, Alec Baldwin, and Samuel L. Jackson, New York Jets owner Woody Johnson, musician Neil Young, comedian Kathy Griffin, rapper Snoop Dogg, fellow businessman-turned-reality-show host Mark Cuban, the entire "highly overrated" cast of *Hamilton,* and fellow celebrity-turned-politician Arnold Schwarzenegger. In fact, Trump has insulted more than 300 people, places, and things via his Twitter account since he announced his candidacy for president in June 2015 (Giannotta, 2018).

SO IF CELEBRITY ENDORSEMENTS WORK, WHY TRUMP?

With the unprecedented amount of celebrity support for Clinton, Trump's election appears to signify a rebuke to pop culture's political influence or does it? Celebrity endorsements were only ineffective on the Clinton side. Trump himself was the celebrity in his campaign. He wasn't a politician, as he had no policy experience and had never held public office. Yet he has been part of the American landscape since the 1980s, which gave him unprecedented name recognition. He was known to voters simply for being a real estate mogul, a popular TV star, and a tabloid media darling. He, with the longest history in entertainment since Ronald Reagan, was the celebrity; and he was the only celebrity he needed.

In a hyper-partisan age, no one, not even celebrities, has the power to convince people to vote. Political cynicism—even when it comes to celebrities—is at an all-time high. In previous elections, celebrity endorsements were less prevalent and the elections less partisan, but when everyone from rappers and pop stars, to Broadway actors and reality show stars, TV and movie actors and basketball and football players to comedians and talk show hosts is speaking out on politics, the noise becomes deafening. And many voters just wanted celebrities to stay in their lanes, especially voters who don't want to hear what any more elites have to say, let alone Hollywood elites who don't understand their plights and whose self-interests are staggeringly different then their own. In 2008, Oprah's endorsement of Obama is estimated to have gotten him a million votes. The fact that she had never endorsed anyone before, and was being broadcast into voters homes every day, added value to her endorsement. Her endorsement of Clinton didn't have nearly the impact because she no longer has the stage of her TV show, and the novelty is gone. Now she is just a celebrity who endorses a candidate in every race.

Celebrities in campaigns have become so commonplace over the last few decades that it's become an expected behavior, and they are now seen as part of the establishment. Their endorsements for Clinton only played into the narrative that she was the establishment. Trump promoted himself as an antiestablishment candidate who bucked the system and eschewed celebrity endorsements. Celebrity disfavor for Trump supported his image as an outsider who was spurned by the country's elite. In the same vein, increased celebrity support may have actually kept the more disenfranchised voters from voting for her, as they were against the system and the system's candidate. This lack of celebrity support, and subsequent lack of ties to the system, fit well with Trump's narrative of "us versus them" and his use of an in-man-out-man-political strategy, where Clinton was the in-man, maintaining the status quo of leaving middle-class Americans behind, and he was the out-man, fighting to make their country great again.

A large portion of Trump's supporters and a key target demographic for his campaign, were people who felt left behind—who felt that he heard them and was targeting them with his promises to return America to greatness. These supporters felt that they and their concerns were invisible to and forgotten by elites, and no one typifies the money, fame, privilege, and status that they are lacking more than celebrities. Trump didn't want celebrities—he didn't need them. Celebrities only further divided the country and alienated the supporters who Trump spoke to—those who felt unseen, unheard, and disrespected. Social media gives celebrities a platform to express their opinions on any issue, but how often do they discuss topics that truly matter to Trump's targeted demographic? Are they discussing income inequality? Loss of industry? Lack of health care? Celebrities may have used social media to post selfies of themselves voting, but at that point, it was just an ego boost attempt to get likes in the virtual echo chambers of their fans. They weren't winning anyone over, informing, or persuading them. They were using it as just another opportunity to draw attention to themselves, further dividing the haves from the have-nots—the privileged from the forgotten. After winning, Trump tweeted, "The forgotten man and woman will never be forgotten again."

Trump supporters have been forgotten in today's pop culture environment. "Roseanne," which went off the air in 1997, was the last time that American television has provided a realistic depiction of what it is like to be a struggling, white working-class family. Celebrities don't even portray them as characters, let alone relate to them as voters. Today, we see niche programming, where gay couples raising adoptive intercultural families, upper-class women doing time behind bars, transgenders as grandparents, interracial families with children who have disabilities—we see all represented in our programming, but the struggling, white, working class doesn't see themselves anywhere in mainstream media. And news media isn't any different. The "coastal elites" don't seem to understand or depict "real Americans," as the two are pitted against each other. After the election, a number of publications, such as the *New York Times*, sent reporters to Middle America in an attempt to determine just who these Trump supporters were, again sending the message that they were idiotic, racist, and uneducated. Similarly representative of the echo chamber concept and this great divide, coastal elites and Middle Americans are out of touch with each other, and celebrity culture is part of one side and neither represents nor speaks to the other. Political commentator, TV host, and comedian Bill Maher explained that no amount of money or celebrity endorsements matter when the Democrats managed to lose this key demographic to their previous successes, the white working man. He said that Democrats made "the white working man feels like, 'Your problems aren't real'"; and that to a lot of Americans, Democrats "have become a boutique party of fake outrage and social engineering. And they're not entirely wrong about that" (Schwartz, 2016).

The 2016 election was about a lot of things, but the underlying issue that the Trump campaign capitalized on was class warfare. In other elections, celebrity endorsements may have worked for many reasons, but in this one, celebrities were the elite, and using them as the voice of one side of the cause only heightened the divide. From the 2016 election, we have learned that celebrities may guarantee a campaign attention, but that can't guarantee votes—especially when the one candidate is a larger-than-life celebrity himself.

REFERENCES

Brennan, D. (2019). "MAGA hats can be symbol of 'tolerance, kindness and inclusiveness'." Says *Fox News*', Laura Ingraham. Retrieved April 26, 2019, from https

://www.newsweek.com/maga-hats-laura-ingraham-donald-trump-racism-xenophobia-fox-news-1314378.

Conley, B. (2018). "Thinking what he says: Market research and the making of Donald Trump's 2016 presidential campaign." In Jamie Gillies (ed.), *Political Marketing in the 2016 U.S. Presidential Election*, pp. 29–48. Cham, Switzerland: Palgrave.

Cosgrove, K. (2018). "Trump and the Republican party refresh." In Jamie Gillies (ed.), *Political Marketing in the 2016 U.S. Presidential Election*, pp. 49–64. Cham, Switzerland: Palgrave.

Elder, E. (2018). "The Clinton campaign: Appeals to moderate swing voters through anti-Trump targeted communication." In Jamie Gillies (ed.), *Political Marketing in the 2016 U.S. Presidential Election*, pp. 81–96. Cham, Switzerland: Palgrave.

Gillies, J. (2018). *Political Marketing in the 2016 U.S. Presidential Election*. Cham, Switzerland: Palgrave.

Hillary for America. (2016). *Jay Z and Special Guests*. Retrieved January 18, 2020, from https://www.facebook.com/hillaryclinton/photos/a.889773484412515.1073741828.889307941125736/1299113203478539/?type=3&theater. Public Domain, https://commons.wikimedia.org/w/index.php?curid=62418696.

Hirsh, M. (2016). *How Trump Rebranded the GOP*. Retrieved March 10, 2019, from https://www.politico.com/magazine/story/2016/03/how-trump-re-branded-the-gop-213745.

Horton, H. (2018). *Trump Dares Oprah Winfrey to Run for President So He Can 'Expose and Defeat' Her*. Retrieved March 13, 2019, from https://www.telegraph.co.uk/news/2018/02/19/donald-trump-ignites-feud-oprah-winfrey-asking-run-president/.

Klein, B. (2018). *Trump Says He Would Defeat Oprah in 2020*. Retrieved March 11, 2019, from https://edition.cnn.com/2018/01/09/politics/trump-oprah-2020/index.html.

Merica, D. (2016). *Jay Z to Headline Concert for Hillary Clinton*. Retrieved March 10, 2019, from https://www.cnn.com/2016/10/24/politics/jay-z-hillary-clinton-concert/.

O'Malley Greenberg, Z. (2016). *Celeb 100: The World's Highest-Paid Celebrities of 2016*. Retrieved March 16, 2019, from https://www.forbes.com/sites/zackomalleygreenburg/2016/07/11/celeb-100-the-worlds-highest-paid-celebrities-of2016/#7ec7a08f56dd.

Oswald, A. (2016). *Here are Hollywood's Biggest Donors in the 2016 Election and How Much They're Spending*. Retrieved March 10, from https://www.businessinsider.com/celebrity-donors-election-2016-3#jj-abrams--502700-to-hillary-clinton-3.

Save the Day. (2016). *The Vids*. Retrieved April 26, 2019, from http://savetheday.vote/.

Siese, A. (2016). *Beyonce: I'm With Her*. Retrieved April 26, 2019, from https://www.dailydot.com/upstream/hillary-clinton-free-concert-jay-z-beyonce/.

Schwartz, I. (2016). *Maher: People Fed Up with "Fake Outrage," "Politically Correct Bullshit" and Response to Islam from Democrats*. Retrieved March 20, 2019, from https://www.realclearpolitics.com/video/2016/11/12/maher_people

_fed_up_with_fake_outrage_politically_correct_bullshit_and_response_to_islam_from_democrats.html.

Skidmore, G. (2016). *Donald Trump Make America Great Again Image.* Retrieved January 17, 2020, from https://www.flickr.com/photos/gageskidmore/25927662706.

Taylor, J. (2018). *Oprah Beats Trump in NPR Pol But Most Americans Don't Want Her to Run for President.* Retrieved March 21, 2019, from https://www.npr.org/2018/01/12/577456987/oprah-beats-trump-in-npr-poll-but-most-americans-dont-want-her-to-run-for-presid.

Zaru, D. (2017). *The Donald Trump-Rosie O'Donnell Feud: A Timeline.* Retrieved March 22, 2019, from https://www.cnn.com/2015/08/07/politics/donald-trump-rosie-odonnell-feud/index.html.

Chapter 6

Celebrities Post-2016

Everyone Is "Woke"

With its celebrity candidates and endorsements, Election 2016 may have seemed like a peak year for the role of celebrity in American politics, but as we have moved beyond 2016, we have only seen celebrity involvement grow. In the past, it was a novelty to see the politically active celebrity, and the audience took notice. Post-2016, it has become an expectation related to fame. It is more noticeable when a celebrity does not stand up for a cause, as it is now more than a norm—it's becoming a civic obligation associated with fame. Voters want more than political candidates. As we saw in 2016, they want a movement—a revolution. In movement politics, it's the ideology that is powerful, not a candidate. The ideas need to be diffused for the movement to grow, and, with their stage and followers, celebrities are the perfect medium to perpetuate and grow a movement's political message. Celebrities have a large amount of resources, both money and attention, which, if applied correctly to a political movement, can generate a lot of attention and progress.

In today's political environment, celebrity activists fall into one of four groups (with some overlap). First, the lifers, such as Susan Sarandon, Tim Robbins, and Roseanne Barr, have been in the public eye for decades and have always been politically vocal. For this group, activism isn't a post-2016 fad; rather, they've spent their careers voicing their political opinions, despite those opinions sometimes negatively impacting their career successes. Second, Generation Y-Z/social media enthusiasts, such as Chrissy Teigen, John Legend, and Cardi B, are relatively young and new on the celebrity scene, but have skyrocketed in fame, partially due to their high social media presence. This group has defined the concept of being a "woke" celebrity, and they have the Twitter rants and Instagram stories to prove it. Third, celebrities who are vocal by necessity, includes people of color, women, and LGBT. These celebrity activists, such as Beyonce, Emma Watson, and

Ellen DeGeneres, use their public position to represent and advocate for their respective groups. They see their role in the public eye as an opportunity to shed light on the issues these groups face, and they believe it is their responsibility to speak out on behalf of the disenfranchised. Fourth, straight white male allies, including George Clooney, Jimmy Kimmel, and Justin Timberlake, are celebrities who see their multitiered privilege as an asset to advocate for those without. While overall this group, white straight males, is often criticized and vilified, these celebrities strive to dispel stereotypes and empower others. They are always demonstrating that, despite their privilege, they "stand with . . . (fill in the blank underrepresented or marginalized group)." Many celebrities fit two or three of these groups, which only strengthens their voice.

Are these celebrities politically active or just politically vocal? Is it activism or opportunism? Prior to the rise of the Black Lives Matter movement, "woke" was a term used only in the black community to be aware of their struggle and daily injustices. A 2008 Erykah Badu song, *Master Teacher*, used the term to recognize that her dream of racial equality was just that, a dream, and then the term virtually disappeared from the mainstream vernacular again. After the 2012 death of Trayvon Martin, woke began resurfacing throughout the Twitterverse, and as the #BlackLivesMatter movement grew, so did woke, including #staywoke, meaning to look past the narrative and examine your own privilege because there is more than one reality in the United States.

Post-2016, celebrities—their music, TV shows, movies, and social media—show a dramatic political shift of social consciousness to one where everyone is woke, meaning to actively be aware of social injustices and prejudices. Are these celebrities leading society in a movement or is it just a fleeting social media moment? And to a generation raised on and empowered by social media, hashtagging, whether its #BlackLivesMatter, #MeToo, #TimesUp, #WeAreTrayvonMartin, #staywoke, or #wokeaf, makes it very easy to appear #woke. Are they truly woke or is it just a pose? To some, celebrity activism appears to be nothing more than self-promotion or likeminded back-patting. It's an opportunity to wear black to show your support of Time's Up or white to show your support of women's economic security. A women's march and cute pink outfit make for a great Instagram photo, and many celebrities have mastered the "look." In 2017, *Vogue* headlined an article: "Zoe Kravitz has the 'Woke' Cool-Girl Look Down Pat" in which they admire Kravitz for providing her followers with an "incredible amount of inspiration lately, in both fashion and politics. In between timely and politically engaging posts, including those from the Women's March in Los Angeles last weekend, there is no dearth of snapshots featuring her laid-back, post-grunge style" (Carlos & Fischer, 2017).

Mainstream culture has a way of commercializing a concept or trend, and then discarding it. And for celebrities, who have both the privilege and freedom to choose silence, when they choose to speak up, it is both morally satisfying and, often, professionally advantageous. It's easy to post a photo or write a song about political angst, but some question if it's enough to say "things are really bad." Is doing so engaging in political activism or just political commentary? And what if they don't partake? Some celebrities' eagerness to engage in social and political conversations has more to do with backlash against those who stay silent.

CELEBRITY POLITICAL ACTIVISM POST-2016: THE "CIVIC OBLIGATION" OF FAME

Trent Reznor versus the "Taylor Swifts of the World"

It has now become so common for an artist to be politically active that it is more likely for them to be criticized when they abstain from politics. It's as if because they are celebrities, they are civically obligated to be politically active, and they are often chastised if they are not. Historically, Taylor Swift has been very vocal about feminism; yet, notoriously apolitical, she remained silent through much of the 2016 campaign, amid the sexual misconduct accusations against Trump. Prior to the 2018 midterm elections, Nine Inch Nails lead singer Trent Reznor, who had previously been quite politically vocal himself against Trump, criticized the pop star and others like her for staying silent "because they are concerned about the brand, their demographic and their success and career" (Reznor, 2018). Reznor argued that celebrities have influence, so it's their job to "call out whatever needs to be called out because there are people who feel the same way but need someone to articulate it" (Reznor, 2018). Although we mainly talk about celebrities' political activity, Swift, instead, managed to generate attention for not speaking out.

In the 2018 midterm elections, American voters voted in record high numbers, with more than 47 percent turning out to vote (Domonoske, 2018). At the risk of being glass half empty, that also means that 53 percent of voters didn't even vote, which is the league minimum benchmark of political activity, yet we consider that to be a record high number. All Americans aren't politically active, some due to fear of professional repercussions, but others for a myriad of other reasons, and yet we don't expect them to be. However, in 2018, we have an expectation of celebrities that they (a) have clear political opinions, (b) are willing to express those opinions, despite any potential negative consequences, and (c) are able to do so in an eloquent manner.

Although I, too, appear apolitical, and I often use the old 2004 Tim Russert quote "I know what the conservatives think, what the liberals think, what the Democrats think, what the Republicans think, and I try to master both sides of an issue to a point where I'm totally confused as to what I think," I actually do have my own clear political opinions, and, hopefully after nearly six chapters, you believe I could eloquently express those opinions. However, I often don't. I vote, of course, as well as take part in other moderate (i.e., "safe") political activity, but for both personal and professional reasons, I often prefer to keep those opinions to myself.

I teach political communication courses, and our projects often lead me to work with local government leaders and political candidates, as well as the local media. The most basic political activity, such as displaying a yard sign, or the simplest social media post could damage years that I have invested in cultivating these relationships. Although I'd like to believe that professional relationships would sustain for the greater good, I also am not naïve enough to believe that I could be much of a political contrarian before I'd begin to see the consequences. Similarly, I have students who range from the most liberal Democrats to the most conservative Republicans. Some of these students are part of the group of political hard cores who have no problem expressing their political opinions even in the face of controversy. However, I have others who shut down if faced with people with opposing viewpoints. It's my job to open these students up to the world, not shut them down. A trend I've seen in my classes post-2016 is the "I could never have a relationship or respect someone who believes or supports X." This works to my advantage if they agree with me, but sets up a hostile learning environment if they don't. And that's just the professional side.

Although I spend my professional life in liberal academia, I spend my personal life immersed in upper-middle class, Catholic School family, Southern Conservative suburbia. These are often two very different politically oriented worlds, and similar to the negative potential to impact aspects of my career, there exists the same potential to negatively impact the social worlds I inhabit if I voice a controversial position or take part in a certain political activity. How would my friend-colleagues respond if I attended a March for Life rally with my children's school? How would my neighbor friends/children's school friends' families respond if I flew a gay pride flag in support of my LGBT friends? So professionally and personally, I have a brand: a brand that I have worked diligently to cultivate over the last forty-three years; a brand that somehow successfully blends and mingles the diversity of who I am. And that brand is very valuable to me—too valuable to risk damaging it simply to go on a Twitter rant. Although I place a high value on things like my children's friends' families inviting us to events and getting student evaluations that say I create a comfortable environment for civic discourse, it is not valued at $320 million, which happens to be Taylor Swift's net worth.

Yes, Trent Reznor, Taylor Swift has a brand—a brand that she has worked diligently to cultivate since she started off as a country singer (which means some of her demographic started off with her during her country-music beginnings) at just fourteen years old. A brand that has garnered her a net worth of $320 million. She does have a platform for influence. On a smaller scale, we could say the same about me. I have a pulpit, a platform for influence, from which to share my political ideas with my students, as they are a captive audience for two and a half hours each week. I could take advantage of this and use this time to "call out whatever needs to be called out." I also straddle two social worlds, so I have the potential to influence both and to bridge certain gaps between. But do I have the civic obligation to do so? Does Taylor Swift? Do other celebrities? Is it my civic obligation to risk my brand? Trent Reznor seems to think so.

And for him, and many other celebrities, it's an easy obligation to fulfill. As the primary member of Nine Inch Nails, an alternative rock band, Reznor produced controversial shock-musician Marilyn Manson's first album and recorded music in a studio housed inside the house where the 1969 Charles Manson murders took place. Whereas Swift has built her brand around the pop-sweet chronicles of her love life, Reznor has built his brand on darkness, shock, and controversy. Not only will he not be negatively impacted by a controversial political position, it will only further his brand image. Other celebrities fall into similar situations, if their brand is based on overcoming obstacles or defying the odds or bucking the system, being politically controversial only helps them perpetuate that brand. LeBron James has built his brand around his image as "just a kid from Akron." He used his talents, and through hard work and determination, he came from nothing. He grew up in the inner city, in a less than stable single-mother home. He rose from the shallows of an underprivileged African American community, and he wants to support others to elevate themselves too. He has the fame. He has the fortune. He has the platform and the influence. He may live in a $23 million mansion in Brentwood, but his brand is "just a kid from Akron." So when LeBron calls Trump a "bum" or supports championship teams' refusals to visit the White House, it isn't a risk for him. Despite his $485 million net worth, his career will not suffer. His demographic won't punish him. But all celebrities do not fit this model, so to expect all celebrities to buck the system, as a civic obligation, is an egregious generalization.

Although not bucking the system entirely, a few months later, right before the 2018 midterms and immediately following the confirmation of Justice Kavanuagh to the Supreme Court, Taylor Swift did break her political silence. Swift is a member of both the second (i.e., Gen Y-Z/social media influencer) and third (i.e., woman) celebrity activist groups, so she used her Instagram to do so. She posted a passionate plea against a Republican candidate for Tennessee Senate, citing the (female!) candidate's record on LGBTQ and women's rights, subsequently endorsing Democratic candidates for Tennessee House and Senate. Overshadowing her candidate endorsements, however, was her overall plea urging her fans to vote in the midterms. Vote.org noted an unprecedented amount of voter registrations after Swift's post, up 65,000 registrations in the following twenty-four-hour period, with a particularly high spike in voter registration in Tennessee (Nechamkin, 2018). Even the vote.org site saw an increase in the number of new visitors, with ten times the number than on a typical day (Nechamkin, 2018). Despite her clear influence, Swift, however, hasn't jumped any further into the political arena. Perhaps her notoriety for being apolitical was the reason that fans took notice and acted when she was. Perhaps celebrities who make politics part of their brand are less influential than one who only dips her toe in periodically. Was the criticism of her silence unfair? Was it actually her civic duty to do so or could she have remained apolitical?

The Dolly Brand

Some stars have incorporated being apolitical into their brands. Country-music legend Dolly Parton has always been one celebrity who tries to stay out of politics, even when others try to force her in. In 2016, she made a comment about supporting a woman in the White House, which was taken as a Hillary Clinton endorsement. Parton clarified and made light of it by releasing the statement, "I have not endorsed Hillary Clinton nor Donald Trump. I try not to get political but if I am, I might as well just run myself 'cause I've got the hair for it, it's huge, and they could always use more boobs in the race." The closest she got to getting involved in the 2016 race was saying that she thought the candidates were "both nuts" and were only out to scare the public about everything: "People just want to have a feeling of security" (King, 2016). In the earliest stages of 2020 campaigning, Parton was quick to deny a candidate's request to use her song *9 to 5* to kick off a presidential bid. To explain that it wasn't a partisan denial, Parton's people stated that they simply do not approve any requests of a political nature (Carlson, 2019).

Not only does Parton not want to endorse candidates in any way, she doesn't even like to be political by association. At the sixty-ninth annual Emmy awards in 2017, Parton found herself on stage and camera between politically vocal, *9 to 5* costars Lily Tomlin and Jane Fonda as they, like many stars that evening, used the event as an opportunity to bash Trump. Parton looked uncomfortable and remained politely silent, although her facial expression couldn't mask her discomfort. In an era of the woke celebrity, Parton has made being apolitical part of her brand. It's not that she doesn't have her political opinions; she has been vocally Christian, as well as pro-women's and gay rights. After sixty years in the public eye, sixty-four albums, ten movies, and her own theme park, with a net worth of $500 million, Parton realizes that her fan base is one of the most diverse in show business, and feels that she's "not in politics" and, instead, is "an entertainer," and you need "to keep your damn mouth shut if you want to stay in show business" (ABC News, 2018). Just like her hair, her breasts, her twang, and her amusement park, staying out of politics has become part of her brand—a brand she has developed over the years that resonates with the most liberal to the most conservative. After six decades in the business, the Trent Reznors of the world will give her a pass, but stars of the woke generation aren't afforded that luxury. They may just be "entertainers," like Parton, but they're from a time when it's seen to some as a civic obligation to use their influence to "call out whatever needs to be called out," even if it means damaging their brand and alienating fans.

Just Shut Up and Dribble: LeBron James

Celebrities can't please everyone. Whereas some people are critical of celebrities for staying quiet, others are critical when they are politically active or vocal, suggesting that doing so abuses the celebrity's status to influence people's opinions regarding important issues. Basically, actors should act, singers should sing, and athletes should just, well shut up and play ball. In early 2018, after basketball stars LeBron James and Kevin Durant criticized President Trump, Fox News host Laura Ingraham proclaimed that they should stick to sports and "shut up and dribble." In response, LeBron defiantly replied that "we will definitely not shut up and dribble." Instead, he used the phrase as the title for a documentary series that he produced, which addresses the evolving role of athletes, specifically through the lens of the NBA, in today's contentious cultural and political environment.

LeBron himself has been one of sports' most influential political and social voices. He had been active both in the movement against racial injustice and as an advocate for providing opportunities to children who come from challenging backgrounds like his own for years prior to 2016. Before we began associating Black Lives Matter with Colin Kaepernick and the NFL, as we'll discuss later in this chapter, LeBron was active in the movement, drawing attention to racial injustice against black men. Protesting the 2012 shooting of Trayvon Martin, LeBron posed with his teammates in a photo wearing hooded sweatshirts, a tribute to the hoodie the teenager was wearing. He captioned it with #WeAreTrayvonMartin and #stereotyped, an expression of solidarity to the boy, who LeBron has said instantly made him think of his own sons, and that it could have been them. Martin's death and subsequent outrage spurred the movement and began the rallying cry that #BlackLivesMatter. In 2014, LeBron, Kyrie Irving, and other NBA players wore "I Can't Breathe" shirts in reference to the last words of Eric Garner, an unarmed black man who died after a police officer placed him in a chokehold. And in 2015, after an infant was killed by gunfire, LeBron took to Twitter to call for gun regulation.

But LeBron has done more than just use social media to start a conversation. He has actively worked to better his community through the creation of the LeBron James Family Foundation and the "I promise" program in 2010. "I feel my calling here goes above basketball. I have a responsibility to lead" (James, 2014). Building off of his brand as "just a kid from Akron," the foundation began gaining attention in 2015 when LeBron partnered with the University of Akron to provide guaranteed four-year scholarships for 1,100 students, costing the foundation close to $42 million. Parallel to his dedication and personalization of Black Lives Matter, LeBron is drawn to helping kids who are in challenging situations similar to his own. "As a kid growing up in the inner city and as an African American kid, you don't really think past high school because it's not possible or your family can't support you. For us to be able to do something like this . . . it means so much" (Windhorst, 2015). The LeBron James Family Foundation also partnered with the Akron Public School District to open the LeBron James I Promise School in 2018, enrolling students who were identified as the worst performers in the Akron public schools and branded with behavioral problems. Although publicly funded, the foundation provided $600,000 for additional training and staff (Windhorst, 2015). After its first year, these children, third and fourth graders who were already labeled as unredeemable, outpaced the rest of the Akron Public School District with their "extraordinary" test-score improvements (Benjamin, 2019). While some may tell LeBron and others like him to just "shut up and dribble," as a political activist and educational philanthropist, he has shown that celebrities can do more.

GIRL POWER: CELEBRITIES LEAD THE WOMEN'S MOVEMENT

#MeToo and Time's Up

In 2016, the United States came closer than ever to making history by electing its first female president. Yet, in the end, the presidency went to a man who, himself, has faced numerous allegations of sexual harassment and sexual misconduct. Although Clinton didn't make history, post-2016, women have. The day after Trump's inauguration, January 21, 2017, the first Women's

March on Washington occurred, a march to both protest his election and call attention to women's issues and women's rights. Subsequent marches were held all over the country, and with over 3 million marchers, it was one of, if not the largest, protests in our history (Morris, 2018). Numerous celebrities were visible at events throughout the country, protesting, speaking, and performing. Emma Watson, Shonda Rhimes, Scarlet Johansson, and America Ferrara were only a few of the celebrity speakers who demanded equality. Performers like Madonna, Samantha Ronson, and the Indigo Girls entertained crowds and made the protest even more of a special event. Celebrities used the marches as a way to be heard, lending the cause their names, their faces, and their social media followers.

But it was later that year, when the women's movement really saw the power of celebrities and their social media, as Alyssa Milano inadvertently reinvigorated a movement and hashtag with one tweet to her millions of followers. Milano asked her followers: "If you've been sexually harassed or assaulted write 'me too' as a reply to this tweet." More than 66,000 replied, opening the floodgates, as women took to social media with their stories and the #MeToo hashtag. Numerous celebrities followed Milano's lead, sharing their own stories of sexual misconduct, or just adding their own #MeToo.

Although women across the world weren't yet using the hashtag, sharing their stories, or creating an online community of support, the #MeToo movement had been around for years. Activist Tarana Burke initially used #MeToo in 2006, also founding a nonprofit organization, Just Be, Inc., which supported the victims of sexual misconduct (Langone, 2018). Although Burke and Just Be, Inc. helped many since 2006, #MeToo didn't become a worldwide social phenomenon until it gained celebrity traction, and the public attention that comes with it, over a decade later. *TIME* magazine named the Silence Breakers of the #MeToo movement as their 2017 Person of the Year, honoring the cause and all of its women, including the celebrities, such as Milano, Ashley Judd, and Taylor Swift, who possessed an unprecedented ability to promote change.

Just as *Time* magazine recognized the cultural shift led by the #MeToo conversation, journalists from media outlets, such as the *New Yorker* and the *New York Times,* also took notice of the stories of sexual misconduct, leading with investigative journalism and the outing of sexual abusers, such as Hollywood's own Harvey Weinstein, drawing attention to how widespread sexual misconduct is, in Hollywood and beyond. Whereas #MeToo focuses specifically on creating a community of women who bond in empathy and share in stories of sexual violence, a group of over 300 women in Hollywood initiated the Time's Up movement as an action-oriented next step to create change, equality, and safety in the workplace (Langone, 2018). Led by celebrities like Reese Witherspoon, Shonda Rhimes, and Natalie Portman,

Time's Up's focus is on getting legislation passed and policies changed. The Time's Up Legal Defense Fund is the source for funding the movement, and celebrities have been at the helm. Beginning with an attention-getting demonstration of unity by most celebrities, male and female, as they dressed in all black and wore Time's Up pins at the Golden Globe Awards, the legal fund was launched. This fund was the most successful GoFundMe campaign to date, as it collected $21 million in the first two months, with a significant majority of the donation's coming from women in Hollywood. Just like their fame, celebrities have the funds, and the friends with the funds, to make a significant financial difference.

Post-2016, the cultural shift has been dramatic, and these once-struggling women's movements can no longer be ignored. Much of that is due to the leadership and influence of celebrities. In a variety of areas, celebrities are taking the lead to push issues to the forefront of the public consciousness, start conversations and advocate against injustice. Celebrities like Lady Gaga, Kerry Washington, and Emma Thompson have been leaders in the work to end violence against women. Lady Gaga disclosed her own sexual assault and began working as an advocate for other survivors. Writing a song, "Til It Happens to You" and using her social media, she has worked to push sexual assault to the forefront of the conversation. Relatedly, Kerry Washington has been a long-time voice for ending domestic violence against women. Washington has financially stood behind her cause by designing a limited edition purse, with 100 percent of the proceeds benefiting the National Network to End Domestic Violence. With her millions of social media followers, the collaboration raises both money for and the profile of the cause. Emma Thompson has taken on the cause of working to end human trafficking. She has written essays, starred in PSAs, and was a driving force in the creation of an art exhibit, "Journey," to raise awareness about brutal experiences of women sold through human trafficking into the sex trade.

Like the Time's Up movement, in addition to violence against women, celebrities are fighting against inequalities, whether due to gender, race, or sexual orientation. Beyonce and Shonda Rhimes are two celebrities who, as black women, are in a unique position to see their identities intersect. Not only do they address the injustices they face as women, but they work from the position where their identities between race and gender intersect and overlap, such as income inequality, sexual harassment, the glass ceiling of TV and music production opportunities, and roles for women in entertainment. Other women, such as Taylor Swift and Tina Fey are active in these movements, but Beyonce and Rhimes are advocates for the area where these women's issues intersect with racial injustice. The political commentary in Beyonce's "Formation" video, loaded with female empowerment and cultural identity, sparked a black "girl power" conversation about the unique experience of being a black woman, which is an area often neglected in conversations involving race or gender. Rhimes fights for diversity in the entertainment industry, in roles, opportunities, and recognition of achievements, for women of color, LGBT women, and women over the age of forty, who are currently underrepresented in the entertainment industry. Miley Cyrus also advocates for the LGBT community, its rights and issues. Cyrus moves beyond just championing the cause through her music and social media and started the Happy Hippie Foundation for homeless LGBT youth. These women advocate for all people, regardless of gender, race, or sexual orientation, to be granted the same civil liberties, rights, and opportunities, starting conversations and bringing the issues of intersection among identities to the public attention.

Politics and the City: Gubernatorial-Candidate Cynthia Nixon

Cynthia Nixon, a celebrity who, as a LGBT woman, advocates for this intersectionality and its causes, took her activism to the next level, running for governor of New York in 2018. Although in chapter 4 we covered the natural overlap between Hollywood and political office and those who successfully moved between, not since Shirley Temple Black's 1967 run for Congress have we seen a female celebrity campaign for office. A long-time activist in New York politics, Nixon may not have won the election, but she was a good example of the challenges for a candidate in this area of intersection, who also happens to be a celebrity. The fame of celebrity can be both beneficial and detrimental to a candidate. Because of her fame, Nixon received immediate buzz around her candidacy, with her campaign announcement video causing her name to be the No. 1 trending topic on Twitter within an hour of its release, and by the evening, it had more than 1 million views on Twitter (Goldmacher, 2018). But with this attention comes criticism.

To some voters, it was her celebrity ego leading her into the race, rather than her political convictions. Despite her history of activism, some looked at her political inexperience and painted her as a celebrity who woke up and decided that she could do a better job at politics than a politician. In response, Nixon's campaign strategy was to try to alter voters' ideas about who celebrities are—rich, coddled, image-obsessed, out of touch with "regular" people, as well as to attack notions about "experience" and how much experience a candidate needs to govern. Not only did Nixon face the challenges of being a woman and a celebrity, but she also is LGBT, married to a woman and identifying as bisexual. Her opponent successfully attacked her on both fronts, even saying that due to her Hollywood credentials, she lived in a "world of fiction," a world in which she imagined governing New York, as her *Sex and the City* character would have, and a world in which she is even an "unqualified lesbian," dismissing her bisexuality, having previously been married to a man.

CELEBRITIES BOYCOTT!

NFL Boycott: Black Lives Matter

Not only do celebrities draw attention to social injustices and spark conversations, but they also lead in action. One social injustice that we've seen celebrities take on post-2016 is Black Lives Matter, notably star-quarterback Colin Kaepernick's activism in the movement, and the subsequent NFL boycotts. In the fall of 2016, during the national anthem for an exhibition game, the San Francisco 49ers quarterback took a stance—or rather a knee—in the Black Lives Matter movement. His silent protest was in response to the racial tensions and injustices of the times. Kaepernick, a vocal advocate for racism and human rights, as well as an outspoken critic of Trump, was "not going to stand up to show pride in a flag for a country that oppresses black people and people of color . . . this is bigger than football and it would be selfish . . . to look the other way" (Gajanan, 2016). Like James in the NBA, Kaepernick wasn't the first NFL player to use the field to protest racial injustice. In 2016, five St. Louis Rams players took the field with the "Hands Up, Don't Shoot" pose, representing the Ferguson protests. In this case, the NFL maintained that the players had the right to exercise free speech (Gajanan, 2016) (figure 6.1).

Although not the first celebrity athlete to make a statement in support of racial injustice, the responses to Kaepernick's statement, both from fellow players and the public, were extreme and diverse. After his initial protest, the 49ers issued their own response, sitting the quarterback out for another preseason game, and stating the value and honor of the national anthem portion of the pregame, while acknowledging their desire to respect the American principles of freedom of religion and expression. The league added that "players are encouraged but not required to stand during the playing of the National Anthem" (Gajanan, 2016). Throughout the season, the NFL found themselves, week after week and game after game, facing more players kneeling in support of both Black Lives Matter and Kaepernick, as well as in opposition to racial injustice. Many players remained standing, some defiantly in protest of the action, but others who found themselves inadvertently making a political statement by standing, just as they had always stood in the past. But now, that stance took on a different meaning. Celebrities joined in solidarity with Kaepernick, and #ImwithKap became a popular hashtag.

Figure 6.1 San Francisco 49ers National Anthem Kneeling. *Source*: Allison, K. (2017). San Francisco 49ers National Anthem Kneeling, CC BY-SA 2.0 Retrieved January 19, 2020, https://commons.wikimedia.org/w/index.php?curid=63402538

The NFL continued to allow players to kneel, and Trump, the celebrity in chief, got involved, calling for his followers to boycott the NFL in opposition to Kaepernick's actions. Trump's boycott emboldened the movement and encouraged more players to participate. As they did, Trump became more adamant in his boycott, calling on the NFL and team owners to fire protesting players.

After a season full of controversy, including the lockout of Kaepernick from playing in the NFL, in May, the league implemented a new policy in an attempt to put an end to the furor. The NFL determined that players would no longer be required to be present on the field during the national anthem; however, those who chose to openly protest on the field could be fined. Social media went crazy in protest of the NFL's decision, and celebrities and activists called for their own boycott. They publicly began pulling their support for the league under the #boycottNFL hashtag. Celebrities criticized the hypocrisy of all that goes unregulated in the NFL while penalizing silent, peaceful protests against social injustice. As Black Lives Matter was at the center of the controversy, the policy only heightened racial tensions. Players threatened sitting out the following season in protest, but they didn't.

The largest visible impact of the boycott came when Rihanna, in a show of support for Kaepernick and in disagreement of the NFL's position, turned down the always-prestigious opportunity to perform in the Super Bowl 2019 halftime show (Darby, 2018). Following suit, through social media, of course, Amy Schumer announced that she was turning down an appearance in a Super Bowl commercial. Cardi B also declined the chance to perform during the show and refused to support the NFL, yet the rapper was featured in a Pepsi Super Bowl commercial. The list grew as Jay Z, Michael B. Jordan, Nicki Minaj, Mary J. Blige, Usher, Lauryn Hill, and many more pulled their support for the event, as well as criticized those who were performing. Amid the initial Kaepernick protest, NFL ratings declined 10 percent during the 2017–2018 season (Berr, 2018). Public interest and memory fades, however, and viewership rebounded, up 5 percent in 2018–2019, as the controversy dwindled. As Rihanna reignited the flame of controversy and celebrities followed suit, Super Bowl 2019 ratings declined to their lowest number in a decade.

Legislative Boycotts: From Georgia to Brunei

Just as celebrities led the two NFL boycotts—first, Trump due to the league's inaction in response to Kaepernick, and second, a slew of progressive celebrities due to the NFL's responsive policy action, celebrities boycott industries based on legislation that they deem unjust. After the Georgia House and Senate passed the 2019 "heartbeat bill," fifty celebrities sent a letter to the governor in opposition. The letter, tweeted out by Alyssa Milano, also included celebrities such as Piper Perabo, Amy Schumer, Rosie O'Donnell, Alec Baldwin, Minnie Driver, Ben Stiller, and more, who signed on, opposing the legislation, which limits the window of time during which women can get an abortion from twenty weeks to six weeks. With a near $10 billion film industry, Georgia is the number one filming location in the world (Hensley, 2017). The actors threatened a financial impact on the state in boycott. The letter states: "As actors, our work often brings us to Georgia . . . . we cannot in good conscience continue to recommend our industry remain in Georgia if H.B. 481 becomes law." These celebrities stand with the Writer's Guild of America, who has threatened to remove all production crews from Georgia, stating that the state would be "an inhospitable place for those in the film and television industry to work . . . many of those in our industry will either want to leave the state or decide not to bring productions there. Such is the potential cost of a blatant attack on every woman's right to control her own body" (Gstalter, 2019).

This isn't the first time that Hollywood has threatened a state due to legislation it deems unjust. In 2016, North Carolina's legislature passed House

Bill 2, a law that revoked some rights to people who are gay or transgender. The film industry in Wilmington, North Carolina, had been booming, earning it the nickname "Hollywood East." The backlash from the bill caused production companies, such as A+E Networks, Turner Broadcasting, and 21st Century Fox to threaten, and end, some productions in North Carolina (Ingram, 2016). The NCAA and NBA also boycotted the bill, moving ACC and NCAA basketball championship games and the 2017 NBA All-Star Game in protest. A 2017 repeal of the bill, and subsequent "compromise bill," repealed portions of the discrimination. Post-H.B. 2, film production is slowly returning to Wilmington and North Carolina, but states like Georgia have been beneficiaries of the film industry boycott and backlash over the bill.

As with state law, celebrities sometimes draw our attention to international legislation that they deem unjust. When celebrities speak, in Georgia or around the world, people pay attention. In 2019, George Clooney penned a guest column in *Deadline*, calling for the immediate boycott of the Beverly Hills Hotel, the Hotel Bel-Air, and six other hotels owned by the Sultan of Brunei. The boycott is in protest of legalization in the small, but very wealthy, country in Southeast Asia, which allows stoning and whipping to death any of its citizens who are proved to be gay. Clooney noted that as a monarchy, a boycott won't itself have an impact on changing the laws, but at least a boycott will keep us from funding the human rights violations, emphasizing that when dealing with murderous regimes, "you can't shame them. But you can shame the banks, the financiers and the institutions that do business with them and choose to look the other way" (Clooney, 2019). He urged his celebrity peers, and others who might find themselves visiting the Beverly Hills Hotel or the Hotel Bel-Air, to take their business elsewhere rather than funding the murder of innocents. Following suit, Ellen DeGeneres tweeted a plea to boycott the hotels, and other stars, such as Arianna Grande and Ellen Pompeo, shared the image.

But this boycott is only renewal of a 2014 Hollywood-led boycott of Brunei's adoption of Islamic Sharia law, which calls for, among other penalties, stoning and amputation for such crimes as theft, adultery, and homosexuality. DeGeneres actively led the boycott then too, as Hollywood fundraisers and Oscar parties were moved from the two Hollywood hotels. But years pass, and attention shifts. Even Clooney, not only a celebrity but also the husband of a human rights attorney, admitted to staying with these hotels recently (Clooney, 2019). Passions may be strong, but attention is often fleeting.

Boycotts and the Issue-Attention Cycle

Celebrity-led boycotts are clear examples of the issue-attention cycle. Public attention shifts from issue to issue on a daily basis, rarely remaining focused on any single social problem for a length of time. Attention and media coverage reflect this public interest, and eventual disinterest. An issue or social problem rises into importance, stays in the public eye for a period of time, and then fades from public attention, though, sometimes, before being solved. Downs (1972) described this repetitive pattern as the issue-attention cycle.

The issue-attention cycle involves the interaction between three groups: the government, the media, and the public. Downs described five stages, varying in duration by issue, but usually occurring in a particular order. The first stage is pre-problem: the issue or condition exists, but it is yet to be depicted in the media and, therefore, is not in the public's attention. Even before 2014, in Brunei, homosexuality was punishable in the country and residents could be sentenced for up to ten years in jail. But the media didn't cover it, so the public didn't know about it, and if it doesn't exist in the public eye, is it really even happening? As a society, we sometimes like to pretend not. The second stage involves the discovery and enthusiasm of the public about a problem. The public gains awareness of a particular problem, which is where our celebrities enter. As we've discussed, celebrities have a platform, a following, media coverage, and the potential to draw a great amount of attention to an issue. They make us aware of the things we would never notice on our own. In 2014, Ellen drew our attention to the injustices of Brunei. We were alarmed. Celebrities joined her, enraged. "This alarmed discovery is invariable accompanied by euphoric enthusiasm about society's ability to 'solve this problem' or 'do something effective' within a relatively short time" (Downs, 1972, p. 39). So we joined her in her boycott. Hollywood boycotted the Hotel Bel-Air and the Beverly Hills Hotel, moving their fundraisers and their fancy parties elsewhere.

However, this U.S. belief that problems can be solved without any essential change to society leads to stage three: realizing the costs. Eventually, reality strikes and the public realize that the costs of the solution are higher than they are willing to endure. Stage four inevitably follows with a gradual decline of interest. "By this time, some other issue is usually entering Stage Two; so it exerts a more novel and thus more powerful claim upon public attention" (Downs, 1972, p. 40). After the 2014 boycott, the 2016 presidential election campaigns began. Our attention shifted. Slowly, imperceptibly, the celebrity boycott softened, and events were booked there again—events attended by LGBT-friendly celebrities, such as Miley Cyrus, Lady Gaga, and Kristen Stewart (Friedman, 2019). Celebrities, and certainly their noncelebrity followers, began to stay there again—even George Clooney. Stage five, the final stage, is an indefinite limbo. At any time, the problem may recapture the public's interest, which is what happened in 2019, when George Clooney brought it back into the media's eye, and subsequent public attention.

Without Clooney's plea, would the United States media even cover Brunei? Would woke celebrities continue to attend events at these hotels? This is the "X factor" that celebrities provide. One letter, one tweet, one image—that's all they need to do. Their followers and media coverage of them are so vast that whether they themselves have the ability to make any change or get any one person to vote a particular way or take action, they have influence. They draw attention and can help craft the media agenda, focusing on the issues that they deem important, which makes those issues the most salient in the minds of society.

THE GOOD, THE BAD, AND THE ODD: ARE WOKE CELEBS CRAFTING THE POLITICAL NARRATIVE?

Captain America Is Launching a Bipartisan (?) Website: Chris Evans

Captain America himself, also known as actor Chris Evans, is stepping into the political arena by launching a website, A Starting Point, aimed at "creating informed, responsible and empathic citizens" (Kurtz, 2019). With well over 10 million Twitter followers, Evans, who would primarily be classified as part of the second type of celebrity activists—although he classifies as part of the fourth group as well, is an avid social media user who has been an outspoken critic of Trump. While acknowledging his concern about the possibility of alienating a portion of his audience and suffering monetary and career damage, Evans said that he would be "disappointed in himself" if he didn't speak up (Kurtz, 2019). But would his 10 million followers be disappointed too? And will they follow him to this new platform? He has the Washington connections to give them something to see, and he intends to use his site as a medium to "demystify politics" by showcasing both Democrat and Republican lawmakers, providing them a platform to present their positions on political issues (DeCosta-Klipa, 2019). Traditionally, this has been the role of mainstream media, but mainstream media doesn't draw 174 million viewers in 1 day (as did the first *Avengers: Infinity War* trailer); Captain America does (Arkin, 2018). This is the fan factor that celebrities like Evans provide. Although attempting to create bipartisan civil discourse, Evans is heading into the project with a clear angle, stating, among other things, that "Trump's an absolute dumb shit" (Kurtz, 2019). Prior to the intended launch of this website, Evans had only voiced these opinions on social media where he received likes and retweets, but A Starting Point is taking it further, moving from being politically vocal to politically active. He has the opinions; he has the followers; he has the connections; and now, he has the platform to be an influential player in Washington.

This begs the question of if celebrities can have more of an impact if they focus on the issues rather than the partisanship. Would Evans' impact on bettering the world through creating "bipartisan civil discourse" be more influential and seem to be more legitimate if he appeared himself to be bipartisan? Statements like "Trump's an absolute dumb shit" are clearly loaded and immediately alienate half of the voters—half of his target audience. When one half is eliminated, there's no discourse, so there's no way for him to be successful. If Evans and other celebrities are truly concerned about bettering the world, solving problems, eliminating injustice, and creating civil discourse, they must actively target a bipartisan audience. The 2016 election demonstrated that celebrity isn't enough for candidate endorsements, but they do draw attention and have a multitude of resources that can be highly beneficial, especially given the theory behind it, as we discussed in part I. When celebrities remain bipartisan, they speak to their fans. When celebrities call Trump a "dumb shit" and the like, they speak to the fans who feel the same as they do. Yes, he can create civil discourse among likeminded individuals, but that's a fairly easy task—a task that doesn't bridge any gaps. Rather, focusing his resources on the issues, and removing his own partisan rants, legitimizes his cause and opens his fans up to amicable discourse. Just as I remove my politics from my classroom discussions to create an environment conducive to civil discourse, if celebrities wish to facilitate open bipartisan dialogue, they must avoid creating a hostile environment for anyone who disagrees with them.

Off with His Head: Kathy Griffin Takes It Too Far

Comedian Kathy Griffin is no stranger to controversy and outrageousness. Prior to 2016, Griffin, who made a career of being a D-list celebrity, had stripped on national television and denounced Jesus at the 2007 Emmy Awards, saying he had nothing to do with her winning the award: "All I can say is, 'Suck it, Jesus.' This award is my God now." If she was that hard on Jesus, you can imagine she didn't go easy on Trump during the 2016 election. A Clinton supporter, Griffin was one of the many celebrities who proclaimed that if Trump was elected, she was moving to Canada. She consistently referred to Trump's election as "a funeral for our Nation." But Griffin is an outspoken comedian, and many celebrities were lashing out with their frustrations.

In May 2017, however, Griffin took her political position against Trump too far, when she staged a photo shoot in which, straight faced, she held up a fake, decapitated Trump head, dripping in blood. Intended as a satire, the image rapidly spread through social media, causing a backlash of anger and disgust all across the political spectrum. Democrats, Republicans, the media, and Trump's family were outraged. Trump tweeted that his eleven-year-old son was having a difficult time dealing with the image, and the Trump family launched a public campaign against Griffin. Immediately, the U.S. Department of Justice and the Secret Service opened investigations on Griffin on suspicion of conspiracy to assassinate the president. As she saw her attempt at humor backfire, Griffin apologized for the image, saying in a video that she "crossed the line . . . and was wrong. . . . It wasn't funny. I get it," adding that it was "too disturbing" (Marikar, 2019).

Her apology didn't suffice. All was not forgiven. Death threats poured in. CNN and Bravo cut ties with her. She was dropped from an endorsement deal, and fifteen live performances were cancelled, due to bomb threats. Griffin estimates it cost her more than a million dollars (Marikar, 2019). Seemingly unemployable, Griffin claimed that Trump "broke her" (Chan, 2017). But it was more than Trump; the public outrage showed that the people had a line. Although at times, that line seems very blurred, especially when it comes to celebrities, it does exist, and Griffin had crossed it. Defiantly, Griffin stopped apologizing. Two years after the infamous photo, despite a lackluster career and remaining death threats, Griffin says she doesn't regret it; she embraces it as her "Hanoi Jane" moment, and she even self-financed a movie "Kathy Griffin: A Hell of a Story," telling her story post-photo (Moniuszko, 2019). But just how short is the public consciousness? Yes, Griffin's brand is humor, sarcasm, controversy, and outrageous acts, but the public still has a say in determining where the line is and punishing celebrities if they cross that line.

An Empire Falls: Jussie Smollett

The public was very clear on where that line was for actor/celebrity political activist Jussie Smollett, after he was allegedly attacked in 2019 in Chicago, seemingly a hate crime victim. Smollett was an admired celebrity voice, drawing attention to racial justice and LGBT equality issues. He was an actor who was not only a celebrity political activist, but people saw him as a role model, positive example of how to be black, gay, and proud in Hollywood. Smollett reported to police that he had been attacked in downtown Chicago by two white men, wearing MAGA hats, who yelled racial and homophobic insults at him, punched him, poured a chemical substance over him, and tied a rope around his neck. The public was shocked that such an atrocious attack would happen. Rallies were held, and celebrities posted their horrified thoughts that this could happen to anyone, let alone their beloved colleague. Smollett drew empathy from both black and gay communities.

But then the story started to get strange, as details emerged that indicated that Smollett himself was behind the alleged attack. As it became clearer that it was a hoax, and the Chicago prosecutor's office got involved, the public became outraged that they had been betrayed. Not only did Smollett discredit himself, but as an activist, he discredited hate crime victims and a false legitimacy to those who already dismiss racism and homophobia. This is the downside of celebrity activism. Celebrities drawing attention to a cause is typically a good thing, but when they do something bad, the negative attention is transferred to the cause as well. In chapter 1 we talked about the halo effect, and how all of the good from a celebrity is transferred to the candidate or cause, but that same effect works both ways, and the negative from this betrayal impacts two communities that already face challenges in public perception.

When celebrities like Smollett and Griffin attract negative attention to their political causes, they make us question if, by making civic participation an obligation of celebrity status, are we putting too much responsibility and credibility in the hands of those who have that credibility for things like acting, singing, or playing a sport? Are we allowing woke celebrities to craft the political narrative? We hope that celebrities are activists for the greater good, yet they're entertainers. What happens when they go too far to get a laugh or to draw attention to their cause or to negotiate a salary? The spotlight is on them for better or for worse, and when the worse happens, it negatively impacts the greater good of their cause. Or does the reward that celebrity status brings a cause simply outweigh the potential costs?

Rap Battles and Summits: Donald Trump, Kanye West, Cardi B, and Snoop Dogg

Once in office, Trump has had interactions, some adversarial and others just odd, emerge with the rap community. First, was the odd, as Trump and Kanye West held the summit of all summits in 2017. Quite the media spectacle, after showering Trump with praise and modeling his MAGA hat on social media, the president invited Kanye to the Oval Office to talk about prison reform, but really, the relationship was most beneficial due to Kanye's celebrity and the fact that he guarantees a buzz and attention everywhere he goes. As media opportunities go, he provided all that the White House had hoped for, as Kanye gave cameras, and the public who couldn't look away, a ten-minute soliloquy on everything from hydrogen planes and alternate universes to his takes on slavery (figure 6.2).

Not quite Kanye-level Trump fans, Snoop Dogg and Cardi B instead took a more traditional celebrity route to address their issues with Trump, and staying on brand with their choices of just *how* to say it. Despite a good

Figure 6.2 President Donald Trump and Kanye West. *Source*: Official White House Photo (2018). President Donald Trump and Kanye West. Retrieved January 18, 2020, from https://www.whitehouse.gov/wp-content/uploads/2018/10/POTD-October-11-2018.jpg, Public Domain, https://commons.wikimedia.org/w/index.php?curid=74124092

relationship during Trump's pre-political years, post-2016, Snoop has been a consistent adversary of Trump, in social media as well as in his music. His 2017 album "Make America Crip Again" features cover art that appears to show a dead Trump (he has a toe tag), draped in an American flag, and the video for his song "Lavender" shows the execution of a clown dressed as Trump. During the 2018 government shutdown, Snoop took to his Instagram to share his thoughts, using some choice words to tell the public that Trump doesn't care about government workers and to encourage voters, especially those government employees, to not vote for Trump in 2020: "Don't vote for that nigga. Please don't. Look what he do. He just don't give a fuck."

In a similar fashion, Cardi B also voiced her opposition of Trump, as well as her sympathy for furloughed government workers, through her Instagram. "This shit is really fucking serious, bro. This shit is crazy. Like, our country is in a hellhole right now, all for a fucking wall. And we need to really take this serious." Cardi B did recognize her limitations as an entertainer, however, adding, "I feel like we need to take some action. I don't know what type of action, bitch, because this is not what I do." Cardi B and Snoop Dogg are certainly woke, and their political commentary does suggest that "Wow! Things are really bad!" but there is a difference between woke social commentary and political activism. Sometimes, celebrity activists, such as LeBron James and Alyssa Milano, do know what needs to be done and just how to get there, but other times, celebrities aren't quite as sure; they just feel that the situation is bad, and they want to use their platforms to draw attention to it. And sometimes, they're only there for the sales, the photo opps, the Instagram likes, and the media attention. The closer we get to election 2020, the more we see . . .

CELEBRITY CASE STUDY: *BRANDING OF THE MARIJUANA INDUSTRY*

One political area that celebrities have been active in for decades is the area of legalization of marijuana. As the legal marijuana industry grows across the country, these celebrities are seeing their activism make legislative strides. In chapter 1, we discussed brand. Every business, organization, and person has a brand. A brand is the overall impression presented outward; it is how people identify, know, remember, and distinguish you from others. Celebrities have brands. Just as Taylor Swift's brand, while feminist, is more pop-sweet relationship narrative than social justice reform, and LeBron James' brand is basketball star, racial injustice advocate, and educational philanthropist, Snoop Dogg's comments and artistic attacks on Trump fit his Doggfather brand, black urban culture, explicit lyrics, slurred social commentary, and "touchin that real STICKY ICKY ICKY." After seamlessly incorporating illegal use of marijuana into his brand over the last twenty years, Snoop and other pot-smoking celebrities, such as Willie Nelson, Cheech and Chong, and Melissa Etheridge, are lending their brands to—and financially cashing in on—the legal marijuana boom.

Just as Nike and Wheaties have used celebrity athlete brands to sell their products for decades, in its early stages of launch and branding, the legal cannibas industry is hoping that they can extend marijuana's appeal beyond traditional stoners and attract a new type of consumer, and they think that celebrity endorsements are the way to do so. Snoop and Willie Nelson type celebrities, who have been long advocates of marijuana and individual rights to use it, provide an authenticity to the brand. But these celebrities aren't just lending their brands to the product; they are creating the brand off of themselves. Bob Marley's family has created Marley Naturals, Willie Nelson has Willie's Reserve that he labels as "born of the awed memories of musicians who visited Willie's bus after a show," and Snoop, the apparent King of the Marijuana industry, has developed an eight-strain line of weed that he calls "Dank from the Doggfather Himself."

REFERENCES

Allison, K. (2017). *San Francisco 49ers National Anthem Kneeling, CC BY-SA 2.0.* Retrieved January 19, 2020 https://commons.wikimedia.org/w/index.php?curid=63402538.

Arkin, D. (2018). *"Avengers: Infinity War" By the Numbers.* Retrieved April 7, 2019 from https://www.nbcnews.com/pop-culture/movies/avengers-infinity-war-here-let-s-look-it-numbers-n869316.

Benjamin, C. (2019). *LeBron James' I Promise School Sees "Extraordinary" Test Score Improvement after First Year.* Retrieved April 10, from https://www.cbssports.com/nba/news/LeBron-james-i-promise-school-sees-extraordinary-test-score-improvement-after-first-year/.

Berr, J. (2018). *The NFL's Ratings Probably Will Continue to Decline.* Retrieved April 6, 2019 from https://www.forbes.com/sites/jonathanberr/2018/08/28/the-nfls-ratings-probably-will-continue-to-decline/.

Carlos, M., & Fischer, S. (2017). *Zoë Kravitz Has the "Woke" Cool-Girl Look Down Pat.* https://www.vogue.com/article/zoe-kravitz-ovo-revenge-politics-big-little-lies-instagram.

Carlso, A. (2019). *Sorry, 2020 Candidates: Dolly Parton Doesn't Like Any of You Using Her Music.* Retrieved April 14, 2019 from https://people.com/politics/2020-presidential-candidates-using-dolly-parton-songs/.

Chan, M. (2017). *"He Broke Me." Kathy Griffin Says Trump Family Ruined Her Life Over Controversial Photo.* Retrieved April 16, 2019 from http://time.com/4803225/kathy-griffin-trump-photo-head/.

DeCosta-Klipa, N. (2019). *Here's Why Chris Evans was Meeting with Ed Markey and Other Members of Congress on Capitol Hill.* Retrieved April 4, 2019 from https://www.boston.com/news/politics/2019/04/08/chris-evans-a-starting-point-politics-website.

Downs, A. (1972). Up and down with ecology—The "issue attention" cycle. *Public Interest, 28,* 38–50.

Finn, N. (2019). *Jussie Smollett's Inspiring Story Gets Complicated: Inside His Road to Empire.* Retrieved April 28, 2019 from https://www.eonline.com/news/1010057/more-than-good-enough-inside-jussie-smollett-s-inspiring-road-to-empire.

Friedman, R. (2019). *LGBTQ Boycott of Beverly Hills Hotel is Revived after Celebs like Miley Cyrus, Kristin Stewart were Unwittingly Guests at Recent Events.* Retrieved April 17, 2019, from https://www.showbiz411.com/2019/03/30/lgbtq-boycott-of-beverly-hills-hotel-is-revived-after-celebs-like-miley-cyrus-kristen-stewart-were-unwittingly-guests-at-recent-events.

Gajanan, M. (2016). *Colin Kaepernick and a Brief History of Protest in Sports.* Retrieved April 18, 2019 from http://time.com/4470998/athletes-protest-colin-kaepernick/.

Goldmacher, S. (2018). *Cynthia Nixon Enters Race for New York Governor.* Retrieved April 19, 2019 from https://www.nytimes.com/2018/03/19/nyregion/cynthia-nixon-new-york-governor-cuomo.html.

Greene, E. (2019). *LeBron James Opens School in his Hometown.* Retrieved April 20, 2019 from https://www.nytimes.com/2019/04/12/education/LeBron-james-school-ohio.html.

Harwood, E. (2018). *Kanye West and Donald Trump take Chaos Mainstream in the Oval Office.* Retrieved April 28, 2019 from https://www.vanityfair.com/style/2018/10/kanye-west-and-donald-trump-take-chaos-mainstream-in-the-oval-office.

Hensley, E. (2017). *Georgia's Film Industry Generates $9.5 Billion Economic Impact in Fiscal 2017.* Retrieved April 13, 2019 from https://www.bizjournals.com/atlanta/news/2017/07/10/georgias-film-industry-generates-9-5-billion.html.

Ingram, H. (2016). *Film Companies Threaten to Boycott NC Unless HB2 Repealed.* Retrieved April 14, 2019 from http://wilmonfilm.blogs.starnewsonline.com/17500/film-companies-threaten-to-boycott-nc-unless-hb2-repealed/.

King, A. (2019). *Dolly Parton on 2016 Candidates: "I Think They're Both Nuts."* Retrieved April 15, 2019 from https://www.cnn.com/2016/08/26/politics/dolly-parton-presidential-candidates/index.html.

Kurtz, J. (2019). *Chris Evans Plans Politics Website "To Create Informed, Responsible and Empathetic Citizens."* Retrieved April 16, 2019 from https://thehill.com/blogs/in-the-know/in-the-know/436049-chris-evans-plans-politics-website-to-create-informed.

James, L. (2014). *The Essay.* Retrieved April 9, 2019 from https://www.si.com/nba/2014/07/11/LeBron-james-cleveland-cavaliers.

Langone, A. (2018). *#MeToo and Time's Up Founders Explain the Difference Between the 2 Movements—And How They're Alike.* Retrieved April 19, 2019 from http://time.com/5189945/whats-the-difference-between-the-metoo-and-times-up-movements/.

Marikar, S. (2019). *Can Kathy Griffin Come Back from the Dead?* Retrieved April 14, 2019 from https://www.newyorker.com/magazine/2019/03/25/can-kathy-griffin-come-back-from-the-dead.

Minichiello, M. (2017). *Taking a Knee for Equality.* Retrieved April 26, 2019 from https://www.dailycamera.com/2017/11/17/michael-minichiello-taking-a-knee-for-equality/.

Mochizuki, K. (2017). *Snoop Dogg's Anti-Trump Album Cover Bashed by Republicans.* Retrieved April 29, 2019 from https://www.comicsands.com/snoop-doggs-trump-album-cover-photo-2521066221.html.

Moniuszko, S. M. (2019). *Kathy Griffin Doesn't Regret Trump Photo Despite Backlash, Death Threats.* Retrieved April 14, 2019 from https://www.usatoday.com/story/life/people/2019/03/24/kathy-griffin-doesnt-regret-trump-photo-despite-backlash-death-threats/3263154002/.

Morris, C. (2018). *Here's How Many People Participated in Women's Marches This Year.* Retrieved April 16, 2019 from http://fortune.com/2018/01/22/womens-march-2018-numbers/.

Nechamkin, S. (2018). *Unprecedented Amount of New Voters Because of Taylor Swift.* Retrieved April 5, 2019 from http://www.thecut.com/2018/10/unprecedented-amount-of-new-voters-because-of-taylor-swift.html.

Official White House Photo. (2018). *President Donald Trump and Kanye West*. Retrieved January 18, 2020 from https://www.whitehouse.gov/wp-content/uploads/2018/10/POTD-October-11-2018.jpg. Public Domain, https://commons.wikimedia.org/w/index.php?curid=74124092.

Payton, B. (2017). *At the Emmy's, Dolly Parton's Reaction to Trump-Bashing was All of Us*. Retrieved April 26, 2019 from https://thefederalist.com/2017/09/18/dolly-parton-face-emmy-awards-bashing-donald-trump-says-it-all/#disqus_thread.

Prendergast, E. (2017). *Kathy Griffin Defends Controversial Trump Photo*. Retrieved April 28, 2019 from https://www.newshub.co.nz/home/entertainment/2017/06/kathy-griffin-defends-controversial-trump-photo.html.

Raskin, A. (2018). *Inside LeBron James' Incredible "I Promise" School in his Hometown of Akron: NBA Legend Opens the Doors for Start of Term and Calls It "One of the Greatest Moments of My Life."* Retrieved April 26, 2019, from https://www.dailymail.co.uk/news/article-6006919/LeBron-Jamess-Promise-School-opens-hometown-Akron-help-disadvantaged-kids.html.

Reznor, T. (2018). *Trent Reznor Thinks Artists Should Speak Out*. Retrieved April 5, 2019 from http://www.nytimes.com/2018/06/20/magazine/trent-reznor-think-artists-should-speak-out.html.

TIME Magazine. (2017). *2017 Person of the Year*. Retrieved April 26, 2019 from http://time.com/time-person-of-the-year-2017-silence-breakers/.

Windhorst, B. (2015). *LeBron James: Cavs' No. 1 Priority Should Be Locking in Tristan Thompson*. Retrieved April 9, 2019 from http://www.espn.com/nba/story/_/id/13432927/LeBron-james-tristan-thompson-cleveland-cavaliers-need-back.

Epilogue

As the 2020 election begins its approach, we see celebrities gearing up. In a race between the sitting president/celebrity-in-chief and a field of Democrats with a variety of progressive platforms, which campaign will spark a revolution? During the 2018 midterms, women ran and won races in historic numbers, and celebrities stood behind a slew of candidates, including Rihanna and DJ Khaled's endorsements for Florida governor, Diddy and Oprah's endorsements for Georgia governor, Taylor Swift's endorsements for Tennessee senate, and T.I.'s endorsement ballot for Florida, Georgia, Maryland, and Massachusetts. Beto O'Rourke made such a celebrity impact in his bid for senate, including Beyonce and LeBron wearing his merch, that immediately upon his loss, celebrities such as Alyssa Milano, Olivia Wilde, and Busy Phillips began tweeting "Beto 2020."

However, being a celebrity favorite didn't prove helpful to candidates as they moved into the second half of the campaign. Even with the royal support of the King (LeBron) and the Queen (Beyonce), Beto O'Rourke didn't make it to the "year out" mark. Similarly, Kamala Harris had the most celebrity backers and the highest amount of celebrity campaign contributions, but she also had a lackluster performance in the polls and financial struggles that caused her to end her presidential bid before she reached 2020. At the midway point of the campaign, the frontrunners, Joe Biden, Bernie Sanders, and Elizabeth Warren, have fewer celebrities backing them than one would expect. What role will celebrities ultimately play in the race, amid such powerful issues? As the race enters its second half, celebrities have been looser with their wallets than their brands, contributing early, but waiting to commit with their endorsements until the field narrows. In the meantime, they are staying woke, with their social media as the outlet to prove it. Until the field narrows, they continue to use their tweets to battle Trump and his policies and their Insta stories for photo opps that best demonstrate their political savvy and social consciousness. The effect of social media on celebrity culture and the subsequent impact of this culture on the political climate will be a vast area of study as we move into the 2020s.

Appendix A

"It Doesn't Affect My Vote": A Study of Third-Person Effects of Celebrity Endorsements in the 2004, 2008, and 2012 Elections

During the 2004, 2008, and 2012 presidential elections, presidential candidates had some of the biggest stars in Hollywood at their sides endorsing their candidacy. These celebrities are symbols of support to a candidate, and if voters identify with the celebrities, then the celebrities' supporters would follow suit and back the candidate (Payne, Hanlon, & Tworney, 2007).

In addition to endorsements, celebrities stepped out to help "Rock the Vote" through nonpartisan voter registration efforts. Public Enemy's Chuck D. has long been involved with the twenty-year-old MTV "Rock the Vote" organization. In 2004, 2008, and 2012, MTV had celebrities encouraging the eighteen- to twenty-four-year-old group through commercials, college campus visits, and concerts to get out the vote. More short lived on the campaigning circuit was Sean "P. Diddy" Combs' 2004 Citizen Change campaign, with its slogan "Vote or Die." Although Citizen Change was inactive by 2006, the "Vote or Die" T-shirt was resurrected at the 2012 Democratic National Convention as a "Vote Obama" parody shirt. Young voter outreach campaigns increased voter awareness of their cause.

In 2004, Citizen Change had a 22 percent awareness among the eighteen-plus demographic and Rock the Vote was even higher at 45 percent (MediaVest, 2004). Whereas Citizen Change has consistent awareness across all age groups, Rock the Vote, mainly due to its MTV affiliation, skews to eighteen- to twenty-four-year-olds (MediaVest, 2004). In 2008, Rock the Vote registered 2.6 million voters and had 5.7 million people visit their website (Rock the Vote, 2009). While we cannot be sure that these celebrity-driven campaigns were directly responsible for voter turnout, all of these efforts undeniable played a role in the record-level turnout of young voters, with over 22 million young voters (eighteen to twenty-nine years old) voting in 2008, 2 million more than in 2004 and 6.5 million more than in 2000 (Rock the Vote, 2009). This led to a majority of young people (51%) voting, the highest level since 1972. In 2012, voter turnout for this age group fell to 45 percent (eighteen to twenty-nine years old), lower than 2004 and 2008, but higher than 1996 and 2000 (CIRCLE, 2013). Notably, Obama was most impacted, receiving 2.4 million fewer votes from young voters in 2012 than in 2008 (CIRCLE, 2013).

This study aims to expand on Brubaker's (2011) research on the role of celebrity in the 2004 and 2008 elections and addresses the impact of celebrity endorsements through the perspective of the third-person effects hypothesis, including the 2012 election. As celebrities become eager to get involved in politics and voters increasingly take their political cues from celebrities, it is important to understand the effects of using this campaign strategy on voters.

HYPOTHESES

Based on existing research, two hypotheses were proposed. First, Meirick's (2004) research suggested that, due to social distance, out-group messages led to third-person effects. People believe that their reference groups are less susceptible to the powerful media than out-groups and the public at large. Therefore, the first hypothesis addressed the third-person effect of celebrity endorsements based on social distance.

> *H1*: Endorsements of the out-group candidate will be perceived to have a greater effect on others than on the self.

The opposite effect should occur for endorsements supporting the in-group candidate. Celebrity endorsements supporting the preferred candidate are considered to be desirable. Therefore, it is self-enhancing to receive those messages (Meirick, 2004). The second hypothesis addressed the opposite of the third-person effect, the first-person effect. Closer social distance through reference groups makes people accept media messages.

> *H2*: Endorsements of the in-group candidate will be perceived to have a greater effect on the self than on others.

METHOD

This study focused on the third-person effects of celebrity endorsements in the 2004 and 2008 presidential elections to see if individuals themselves were affected, if they believe others like them (in-group) were affected, if they believe others unlike them (out-group) were affected, or if they believe the public at large was affected by the endorsements.

Data for this study were collected during the 2004 presidential election from 364 participants, during the 2008 presidential election from 253 participants, and during the 2012 presidential election from 352 participants. As reported by MediaVest (2004), 40 percent of young adults eighteen to twenty-four years old were influenced by celebrity endorsements. Jackson (2005) found that young people's level of agreement with political statements made my celebrities increased with their adoration. Specifically, unpopular statements were made more palatable and already popular statements were agreed with more when stated by adored celebrities. Similarly, market research indicates that young adults were influenced by their attachment to celebrities when shaping their sense of identity and their feelings of self-worth (Boon & Lomone, 2006). In addition, celebrity role models influenced young people's brand choices and attitudes toward brands (Bush, Martin & Bush, 2004). Therefore, a college sample was appropriate for study of this trend, as the selling of politicians is often equated to the selling of product brands (Powell & Cowart, 2003).

The participants were undergraduate students enrolled in communication courses. Participants were asked for demographic information, interest in the 2004/2008/2012 presidential campaigns, intention to vote and political affiliation. In addition, they were asked, "if the presidential election were held today, I would vote for . . . ." To allow in-group and out-group classification, participants were omitted if (a) they did not identify themselves as Democrat or Republican, (b) they identified themselves as Democrats for Bush/McCain/Romney or Republicans for Kerry/Obama, or (c) they did not intend to vote in the 2004/2008/2012 presidential election. That left 232 participants for analysis in 2004, 166 in 2008, and 205 in 2012.

The mean age for the 2004 sample was 20.31 ($SD = 4.14$). The sample was predominantly female (62.5%) and white (90.1%). The mean age for the 2008 sample was 21.18 ($SD = 4.23$). This sample was also predominantly female (60.2%) and white (92.3%). The mean age for the 2012 sample was 20.83 ($SD = 4.22$). This sample was also predominantly female (61.6%) and white (92.8%). Political affiliation was split with 45.3 percent Republican and 54.7 percent Democrat in 2004, 47.4 percent Republican and 52.6 percent Democrat in 2008, and 55.1 percent Republican and 44.9 percent Democrat in 2012. In 2004, 79.7 percent intended to vote in the presidential election, with 44.5 percent intending to vote for Bush and 46.4 percent intending to vote for Kerry at the time of the study. In 2008, 88.3 percent intended to vote in the presidential election, with 36.7 percent intending to vote for McCain and 51.6 percent intending to vote for Obama at the time of the study. In 2012, 89.0 percent intended to vote in the presidential election, with 45.0

percent intending to vote for Romney and 44.0 percent intending to vote for Obama at the time of the study. Participants in the 2008 study were more interested in their election (mean = 5.59, SD = 1.47) than 2004 participants were in their election (mean = 4.25, SD = 1.52). Participants' interest in the 2012 election increased even more in 2012 (mean = 5.606, SD = 1.35).

Students were asked to complete paper-and-pencil self-administered surveys. First, participants were asked to provide demographic information, including political affiliation. Second, they were asked about their voting intentions in the 2004 (2008) presidential election. They were asked the question, "If the presidential election were held today, I would vote for" with the response options, George W. Bush/Dick Cheney (John McCain/Sarah Palin; Mitt Romney/Paul Ryan), John Kerry/John Edwards (Barack Obama/Joe Biden), and I will not vote in the 2004/2008/2012 presidential election. In addition, participants were also asked to indicate their likelihood of voting for each candidate with response options ranging from 1 (*strongly disagree*) to 7 (*strongly agree*).

Third, participants were asked to indicate their level of political interest in the campaign. They were given the statement, "I consider myself to be interested in the 2004/2008/2012 presidential election campaign," and provided response options ranging from 1, meaning *strongly disagree* to 7, meaning *strongly agree*. A single-item measure of political interest is the most common way to address the variable in the literature (Bybee, McLeod, Luetscher & Garramone, 2001; Johnson & Kaye, 2003; Kaye & Johnson, 2002; Tedin, 2001).

Fourth, the study examined the third-person effects of celebrity endorsements with a measure adapted from Meirick's (2004) measure of the third-person effects of political advertisements. Participants were told of various celebrity endorsements of both George W. Bush (John McCain/Mitt Romney) and John Kerry (Barack Obama). Endorsements were chosen to represent a broad range of celebrity in equal support of both candidates. Comedian Dennis Miller, singer Jessica Simpson, and actor Bruce Willis endorsed George W. Bush, and actor Martin Sheen, singer Bruce Springsteen, and actor Ben Affleck endorsed John Kerry. Arnold Schwarzenegger, Sylvester Stallone, and Curt Schilling endorsed John McCain, and Oprah Winfrey, Robert DeNiro, and George Clooney endorsed Barack Obama in 2008. Adam Sandler, Trace Adkins, and Jon Cryer endorsed Mitt Romney, and Beyonce, John Legend, and Neil Patrick Harris endorsed Barack Obama in 2012. After each endorsement, participants were asked (a) to rate each candidate on a 7-point Likert-type scale of favorability, with a range of 1 (*very unfavorable*) to 7 (*very favorable*); (b) to indicate whether the endorsement affected their impression of the endorsed candidate on a 7-point Likert-type scale, with a range of 1 (*much less favorable*) to 7 (*much more favorable*); (c) to indicate whether the endorsement affected their likelihood of voting for the endorsed candidate on a 7-point Likert-type scale, with a range of 1 (*much less likely to vote for him*) to 7 (*much more likely to vote for him*); and (d) to predict the effect that the endorsement would have on Democrats, Republicans, and the general public's impression of the endorsed candidate and likelihood of voting for the candidate on 7-point Likert-type scales.

To establish in-group and out-group endorsements, endorsements were combined into two sets of data: Democrat endorsement and Republican endorsement. In an effort to eliminate any personal effect of an individual celebrity's endorsement, the responses for the three Democratic endorsements were combined and averaged. The same was done for the three Republican endorsements. For example, responses to the three questions that asked whether Jessica Simpson's endorsement/Bruce Willis' endorsement/Dennis Miller's endorsement of Bush affected Democrat's impression of Bush were averaged together for a single effect on out-group score for Republicans.

RESULTS

Hypothesis 1 predicted third-person effects for celebrity endorsements of the out-group candidate. To test this, various paired-sample t tests were run on perceived effects of celebrity endorsements of the out-group candidate on perceived effect on self and the public in general, as well as progressively distant others (in-group, out-group). Perceived effects were measured through two variables: effect of the endorsement on the impression of the endorsed candidate and effect of the endorsement on the likelihood of voting for the endorsed candidate.

Hypothesis 1 was consistently supported for both Republicans and Democrats in all three elections studied. Participants of both party affiliations perceived the public to be more affected by out-group candidate endorsements than they were themselves for both their impression of the endorsed candidate and likelihood of voting for the endorsed candidate. In 2004, Democrats perceiving the effects of Republican (Bush) endorsements believed the effects to be significantly greater on the public than on their own likelihood of voting for Bush ($t_{(126)} = -5.258$, $p < .001$) and on the public than on their own impression of Bush ($t_{(126)} = -5.069$, $p < .001$). In 2008, Democrats perceiving the effects of Republican (McCain) endorsements believed the effects to be significantly greater on the public than on their own likelihood of voting for McCain ($t_{(100)} = -5.689$, $p < .001$) and on the public than on their own impression of McCain ($t_{(100)} = -6.202$, $p < .001$). In 2012, Democrats perceiving the effects of Republican (Romney) endorsements believed the effects to be significantly greater on the public than on their own likelihood of voting for Romney ($t_{(90)} = -6.595$, $p < .001$) and on the public than on their own impression of Romney ($t_{(89)} = -6.904$, $p < .001$). In 2004, Republicans perceiving the effects of Democrat (Kerry) endorsements also believed the effects to be significantly greater on the public than on their own likelihood of voting for Kerry ($t_{(104)} = -5.594$, $p < .001$) and on the public than their own impression of Kerry ($t_{(104)} = -5.104$, $p < .001$). In 2008, Republicans perceiving the effects of Democrat (Obama) endorsements also believed the effects to be significantly greater on the public than on their own likelihood of voting for Obama ($t_{(89)} = -7.526$, $p < .001$) and on the public than their own impression of Obama ($t_{(89)} = -7.263$, $p < .001$). In 2012, Republicans perceiving the effects of Democrat (Obama) endorsements also believed the effects to be significantly greater on the public than on their own likelihood of voting for Obama ($t_{(111)} = -7.303$, $p < .001$) and on the public than their own impression of Obama ($t_{(112)} = -8.869$, $p < .001$).

However, when broken up by social distance, results were inconsistent with previous research on social distance. For both Republicans and Democrats, the effect of out-group candidate endorsements was perceived to be greater on the public, the in-group, and the self than on the out-group. In 2004, Republicans perceived Democrat endorsements to have a significantly greater effect on the in-group than the out-group for both impression of Kerry ($t_{(104)} = -6.115$, $p < .001$) and likelihood of voting for Kerry ($t_{(104)} = -5.787$, $p < .001$), a significantly greater effect on the public than the out-group for both impression ($t_{(104)} = -5.165$, $p < .001$) and likelihood of voting ($t_{(104)} = -5.718$, $p < .001$). Republicans perceived Democrat endorsements to have a greater effect on the in-group than the public for likelihood of voting for Kerry ($t_{(104)} = 2.484$, $p < .05$) but not significantly greater for impression of Kerry ($t_{(104)} = 1.609$, $p = .111$). The same results were true for Democrats' perceptions of Republican endorsements.

In 2008, Republicans perceived Democrat endorsements to have a significantly greater effect on the in-group than the out-group for both impression of Obama ($t_{(88)} = -6.322$, $p < .001$) and likelihood of voting for Obama ($t_{(88)} = -7.854$, $p < .001$), a significantly greater effect on the public than the out-group for both impression ($t_{(88)} = -5.562$, $p < .001$) and likelihood of voting ($t_{(88)} = -6.728$, $p < .001$). Republicans perceived Democrat endorsements to have a greater effect on the in-group than the public for likelihood of voting for Obama ($t_{(88)} = 2.568$, $p < .05$) but not significantly greater for impression of Obama ($t_{(88)} = 1.803$, $p = .075$). The same results were true for Democrats' perceptions of Republican endorsements.

In 2012, results were consistent with the two previous elections, but even greater and more significant in a few areas. Republicans perceived Democrat endorsements to have a significantly greater effect on the in-group than the out-group for both impression of Obama ($t_{(111)} = -9.239$, $p < .001$), a notable increase from 2012, and likelihood of voting for Obama ($t_{(111)} = -8.773$, $p < .001$), a significantly greater effect on the public than the out-group for both impression ($t_{(112)} = -7.881$, $p < .001$), a notable increase from 2008, and likelihood of voting ($t_{(110)} = -5.820$, $p < .001$). In 2012 Republicans perceived Democrat endorsements to have a significantly greater effect on the in-group than the public for both impression of Obama ($t_{(111)} = 3.051$, $p < .005$), and likelihood of voting for Obama ($t_{(111)} = 4.935$, $p < .001$). The same results were true for Democrats' perceptions of Republican endorsements.

Hypothesis 2 predicted first-person effects for celebrity endorsements of the in-group candidate. To test this, various paired-sample t tests were run on perceived effects of celebrity endorsements of the in-group candidate on perceived effect on self and the public in general, as well as progressively distant others (in-group, out-group). Perceived effects were measured through two variables: effect of the endorsement on the impression of the endorsed candidate and effect of the endorsement on the likelihood of voting for the endorsed candidate.

Hypothesis 2 was not supported for either Democrats or Republicans in either 2004 or 2008. First-person effect occurred only for one condition. In 2004, Republicans perceived the in-group (Bush) endorsements to have a greater effect on their own likelihood of voting for Bush (self) than on the out-group's likelihood of voting for Bush ($t_{(105)} = 2.145$, $p < .05$, $M = .17$, $SD = .789$). For the remaining conditions, results of the paired-sample t tests substantiated a third-person effect for the in-group candidate's endorsements as well as for the out-group's candidate. However, in 2012, Hypothesis 2 was supported for both Republicans and Democrats on impression of candidate. Republicans perceived the in-group (Romney) endorsements to have a greater effect on their own impression of Romney (self) than on the out-group's impression of Romney ($t_{(110)} = 4.791$, $p < .001$, $M = .29$, $SD = .641$). Democrats also perceived the in-group (Obama) endorsements to have a great effect on their own impression of Obama (self) than on the out-group's impression of Obama ($t_{(91)} = 3.808$, $p < .001$, $M = .24$, $SD = .611$).

DISCUSSION

Looking at this cultural phenomenon over three elections and nearly a decade, overall, this study had three significant findings. First, people distanced themselves from the undesirable messages. Third-person effects were demonstrated in both Republicans and Democrats in that participants felt that the public would be more affected by the opposing, or out-group, candidate's endorsements than they themselves would be in both impression of the endorsed candidate and likelihood of voting for the endorsed candidate.

Third-person effects occur due to self-enhancement. When a persuasive media message is seen as undesirable, a third-person effect occurs. Any endorsement of the opposing candidate, whether through celebrity endorsement or traditional political advertisement, was seen as highly undesirable. Therefore, through self-enhancement, third-person effects occurred.

Second, when broken up into in-group (their political party) and out-group (the opposing, and endorsed candidate's, party), the third-person effect was only significantly greater for the in-group, not the out-group, for both impression of endorsed candidate and likelihood of voting for candidate. Again, this may again be due to the political polarization of the election. Previous researchers found that social distance plays a role in third-person effects. The further the group is from the self, the more susceptible they are to the persuasive message. This was not the case for celebrity endorsements. People recognized the partisanship that existed and knew that most Democrats supported Kerry or Obama, and most Republicans supported Bush, McCain, or Romney, although this party support wasn't as strong in 2008, with many Republicans becoming disheartened with the direction of their party and voting for Obama, yet bounced back in 2012.

The most important implication of this study is that, in an election filled with political polarization, such as these, when people are very strong in their political convictions and often unwavering in support of their presidential candidate and overall, political parties hold their bases, a celebrity endorsement supporting a candidate will not have any room to influence voters' decisions because they are already in favor of the endorsed candidate. The in-group, however, does have the potential to be persuaded by the opposing candidate's endorsements. Keeping in line with the findings of previous research on social distance, in this study, although people knew that they were too knowledgeable to be influenced by the opposing candidate's celebrity endorsement, they were concerned about others, within the general public and their own political party.

Third, the 2012 election study had one significantly different finding than in the previous two elections. The 2004 and 2008 studies did not find first-person effects occurring due to celebrity endorsements. However, 2012 had a very different result. First-person effects were supported for both Republicans and Democrats. First-person effects traditionally occur because people find the message to be desirable, as it supports their point of view. Political advertisements deal with the candidates and their issues. People support both and, therefore, may feel close to the position. However, 2004 and 2008 suggested that the stigma associated with celebrities in politics may have removed any self-enhancement that a supportive message typically holds. Whereas Democrats may have supported Kerry's or Obama's positions and assimilated advertisements that carried their message, they may have seen celebrities' politics as irrelevant and, therefore, distanced themselves from Ben Affleck's political stumping. Although they knew that they were above caring what Ben said, they didn't feel that others were. Therefore, others, in-group or out, are much more susceptible, regardless of the fact that it's in support of their own candidate. It's interesting to see such a dramatic change in 2012.

I suggest two possibilities for this change—one a pedagogical accomplishment and the other a cultural evolution. First, this sample was of college in a Communication Studies department that has expanded our media, political communication, and integrated marketing course offerings and included a vast array of applied experiences in response to a university initiative to promote engaged learning. It's possible that in those four years, our students, the studies' participants, became much more cognoscente of the influence of endorsements and the impact that they truly have. Gone are the days when our students tell us "advertising doesn't affect me. I never buy something because of a commercial." Perhaps they've begun to realize through their studies how influential persuasive messages can be. Second, this generation of college students is very self-aware. They spend their time sharing their lives on social media sites and following, not only their peers' lives, but the same celebrities who are offering political endorsements. The world of social media, with its tweets, retweets, follows, and likes, has changed the way college-age students live and definitely how political candidates campaign. It's possible that these first-person effects are yet another area that social media has shown its impact on politics.

REFERENCES

Boon, S. D., & Lomore, C. D. (2006). Admirer-celebrity relationships among young adults. *Human Communication Research*, *27*, 432–465. Retrieved May 25, 2011 from Wiley Online Library.

Brubaker, J. (2011). It doesn't affect my vote: Third-person effects of celebrity endorsements on college voters in the 2004 and 2008 presidential elections. *American Communication Journal*, *13*(2), 4–22.

Bush, A. J., Martin, C. A., & Bush, V. D. (2004). Sports celebrity influence on the behavioral intentions of Generation Y. *Journal of Advertising Research*, *44*, 108–118.

Bybee, C. R., McLeod, J. M., Luetscher, W. D., & Garramone, G. (2001). Mass communication and voter volatility. *Public Opinion Quarterly*, *45*, 69–90.

CIRCLE. (2013). *The Youth Vote in 2012*. Retrieved March 22, 2014 from http://www.civicyouth.org.

Jackson, D. J. (2005). The influence of celebrity endorsements on young adults' political opinions. *Harvard International Journal of Press/Politics*, *10*, 80–98. Retrieved May 25, 2011 from http://hij.sagepub.com/content/10/3/80.short.

Johnson, T. J., & Kaye, B. K. (2003). A boost or bust for democracy? *Harvard International Journal of Press/Politics, 8*, 9–35.

Kaye, B. K., & Johnson, T. J. (2002). Online and in the know: Uses and gratifications of the web for political information. *Journal of Broadcasting & Electronic Media, 46*, 54–71.

MediaVest USA. (2004, September 30). *Word to Presidential Hopefuls: Celebrities on Campaign Trail Reach Young Voters.* Retrieved March 22, 2005 from http://www.mediaweek.com.

Meirick, P. C. (2004). Topic-relevant reference groups and dimensions of distance: Political advertising and first- and third-person effects. *Communication Research, 31*, 234–255.

Payne, J. G., Hanlon, J. P., & Tworney, D. P. (2007). Celebrity spectacle influence on young voters in the 2004 presidential campaign. *American Behavioral Scientist, 50*, 1239–1246.

Powell, L., & Cowart, J. (2003). *Political Campaign Communication.* Boston, MA: Allyn & Bacon.

Rock the Vote. (2009). *About Us.* Retrieved August 15, 2009 from http://www.rockthevote.org.

Tedin, K. L. (2001). Change and stability in presidential popularity at the individual level. *Public Opinion Quarterly, 50*, 555–562.

Index

advertising, 4, 6–7; and brand messages, 25
AIDS, 11
attribution theory, 35

Badu, Erykah, 80
bandwagon, 25
Barr, Roseanne, 71, 76, 79. *See also* Roseanne
Beatty, Warren, 54; *Bulworth,* 55
Belafonte, Harry, 51–54
Beyonce, 71, 79, 88, 105
Black Lives Matter, 13, 29, 80, 85
Bloom, Rachel ("Holy Shit (You've got to vote)"), 72
Blue Cross/Blue Shield, 5
boycotts, 90–93. *See also* Brunei; Heartbeat Bill; Kaepernick, Colin; NFL
brand, 7–8; brand communication, 7–8; brand development, 7–8; brand identity, 10, 16; and celebrity, 11–13; policy branding, 11; political *branding*, 11; and political movements, 11; and political parties, 11
Brunei, 93–94. *See also* boycotts
Burger King, 5
Burke, Tarana, 87. *See also* Me Too
business-orientation, 7

candidate-driven campaigning, 64
Captain America, 95. *See also* Evans, Chris
Cardi B, 98–99
celebrity, 11–13, 45; and activism, 51–59, 72; and branding, 11–13; as donors, 73; endorsements, 9, 11–12, 38–39, 58–60, 70–71; as heuristic, 29; and parasocial interaction, 34–36; in 2016, 70–75
central route to persuasion (central processing route), 21, 23–24, 26
Chaplin, Charlie, 48–49
civil rights movement, 11, 51; and movement politics, 51
Clinton, Bill, 56
Clinton, Hillary, 63–76; 2016 campaign, 63–76
Clooney, George, 39, 93. *See also* boycotts
commercial marketing, 8–9
communication, 3–4
consensus, 24–25, 28–29
conservative (Conservative Brand), 11
consumer-orientation (consumer-driven, consumer-based strategy), 7, 66, 68
credibility, 10, 12–14, 24–29
Cyrus, Miley, 89

dual-process models, 20

earned media, 66. *See also* free media
Elaboration Likelihood Model, 20–29
elaborations, 20–29
elections: Election 2004, 107–15; Election 2008, 107–15; Election 2012, 107–15; Election 2016, 63–76
endorsements: celebrity, 14–15, 39, 58–60, 70; history of celebrity endorsements, 45; meaning transfer, 13
entertainment TV: and campaigning, 56–59, 66
Evans, Chris, 95. *See also* Captain America

Fonda, Jane, 51–54
free media, 66. *See also* earned media

Georgia, 92–93. *See also* boycotts; Heartbeat Bill
Gestalt theory, 6
get-out-the-vote Rally, 71–72
Great Dictator, The, 48–49
Griffin, Kathy, 96–97

halo effect, 13–14
Heartbeat Bill, 92–93. *See also* boycotts
Heston, Charlton, 51–53
heuristic, 24–29; celebrity as a, 29–30
Heuristic-Systematic Model, 20
Hollywood March, 52
House Bill 2 (HB 2), 92–93. *See also* boycotts; North Carolina

influence marketing, 14
in-group/out-group, 37. *See also* out-group/in-group
Integrated Marketing Communication, 3–4, 6–8, 63–68; 4 Ps and 4 Cs, 68–69; Election 2016, 63–68; IMC and branding, 7–8
involvement: Elaboration Likelihood Model, 24–25; issue, 22
issue-attention cycle, 93–94

James, Lebron, 12–13, 29–33, 70–71, 83–86; I Promise School, 83–86; Lebron James Family Foundation, 83–86

Kaepernick, Colin, 90–92
Kelly, Megyn, 74
King, Jr., Martin Luther, 51
Kravitz, Zoe, 80

liking, 13, 24–25, 27–29; liking and celebrity, 27–29

Maher, Bill, 76
marijuana industry, 100; branding of, 100
marketing, 6–7
Mayer, Louis, 50–51; MGM studios, 50–51
McGovern, George, 54–55
Meaning Transfer Perspective, 13
Me Too, 86–88. *See also* Burke, Tarana; Time's Up
Milano, Alyssa, 87
movement politics, 51–54, 68, 79
Murphy, George, 51

need for cognition: and Elaboration Likelihood Model, 22, 27; and political communication, 25–26
NFL, 90–92. *See also* boycotts; Kaepernick, Colin
Nixon, Cynthia, 89
North Carolina, 92–93. *See also* boycotts; House Bill 2 (HB 2)

Obama, Barack, 5, 70–75, 107
O'Donnell, Rosie, 73–74
out-group/in-group, 37. *See also* in-group/out-group

parasocial interaction, 34–35
Parton, Dolly, 84–85
peripheral: cues, 20–30; route, 20–30
persuasive messages, 20, 24–27

political activism, 48, 81; and celebrities, 48, 81–82; celebrity-driven activism, 48
political awareness, 26
political communication: and Elaboration Likelihood Model, 25–30
political cynicism, 74
political marketing, 8–9, 63–70
political movements, 11, 16; and branding, 16
political parties, 10–11
Pope Pius IX, 47
product-based, 68
public opinion and policy, 5–6
public relations, 4–7

Queen Victoria, 47

Reagan, Ronald, 11, 50–52, 69
rebranding, 16, 69
Republican Party, 69; and celebrities, 50–52
Reznor, Trent, 81
Rhimes, Shonda, 87
Roseanne, 76. *See also* Barr, Roseanne

Sanders, Bernie, 15, 63–69; and celebrity endorsements, 15
"Save the Day" PSA, 72
Schwarzenegger, Arnold, 45, 55–57; Conan the Republican, 55; Governator, 55–57; Shriver/Kennedy, 55
similarity: and persuasion, 25

Smollett, Jussie, 97–98
Snoop Dogg, 98–100; Doggfather, 100
Springsteen, Bruce, 58–60
social distance, 37
social media: #feelthebern, 66; #MAGA, 66; role in political campaigns, 58–60, 63–66, 71–80
social responsibility, 5
Starbucks, 5–6
Swift, Taylor, 81–84

Third-person Effects, 36–39, 107–14; criticism of, 38; and politics, 38–39
Time's Up, 30, 80, 86–88. *See also* Me Too; women's movement
Trump, Donald, 63–76, 81, 84–85, 90–98; and celebrities, 70–74; brand, 67–70; and IMC, 67–69; marketing in 2016, 63–67; Twitter feuds/wars, 73–74
Twitter: Trump feuds, 73–74

Vietnam War, 51–54; and movement politics, 51–54
Vote for Change, 58–59

West, Kanye, 98–99
Winfrey, Oprah, 39, 73–75
Witherspoon, Reece, 13, 29–30, 36
woke, 79–85, 95–100
women's movement, 11, 86–88. *See also* Me Too; Time's Up
Woods, Tiger, 15

About the Author

Jennifer Brubaker, PhD, is an associate professor in the Department of Communication Studies at the University of North Carolina Wilmington. She earned her PhD in political communication and media effects at Kent State University and her master's degree in journalism and undergraduate degree in business from the Ohio State University. At UNCW, Dr. Brubaker teaches primarily political communication, persuasion and integrated marketing communication courses and oversees both the campaign management and journalism programs. She began her research on celebrities and politics during the 2004 election and has published work in political communication in, among others, *Communication Research Reports*, *American Communication Journal*, *Southern Communication Journal*, and *Innovations in Education and Teaching International*.